THE
LUNCHEON
SOCIETY

To Carol

From

[signature: John Hagel]

The Luncheon Society
Journey Beyond Fear
John Hagel III
January 2022

THE JOURNEY BEYOND FEAR

"The global viral pandemic is mirrored by an epidemic of 'zero-sum' fears, false narratives, and plummeting social trust. In *The Journey Beyond Fear*, John Hagel offers an antidote: cultivating our passions within narratives engaging us with people, platforms, and purpose beyond ourselves. It's full of inspiring ideas for those feeling isolated in their working lives, and practical tips for those already tackling complex ecosystem challenges that our societies face."

—**BYRON AUGUSTE,** CEO of Opportunity@Work, former National Economic Council Deputy Director and economic advisor to President Obama

"In this brilliant book, John Hagel clearly proves that the greatest challenge facing us is fear. But more importantly, he shows that there is a way out of that fear by harnessing the passion of the explorer. While other books have described growth mindsets and other upward-looking approaches, John's book goes much further than that. By laying out the path to harness the power of narrative, John empowers us not just to describe the journey in a way that brings others, but to help motivate ourselves deeply, and in doing so unlock the explorer in us all. I am an explorer and I find myself excited and at times challenged by my nature. For explorers who have ever asked, "Why am I doing this?" you'll find John's book to be both vulnerable and insightful as you transmute pressure into opportunity for all."

—**NICHOL BRADFORD,** Executive Director and Co-Founder of The Transformative Technology Lab and Lecturer at Stanford University

"In *The Journey Beyond Fear*, John Hagel masterfully draws on insights from his dynamic career in Silicon Valley and global consulting to demonstrate how institutions and individuals can beat fear and leverage optimism to create thoughtful social innovation. You will be glad you read this book."

—**ARTHUR C. BROOKS,** Professor, Harvard Kennedy School and Harvard Business School, and *New York Times* bestselling author

"The growing challenges in our world are very real, but we need to resist the tendency to become overwhelmed by them. Don't pass up the opportunity to read this inspiring book—it can help all of us to craft an exciting and richly rewarding journey."

—**ED CATMULL,** Co-Founder of Pixar and retired President of Walt Disney Animation Studios

"Fear often disrupts the potential to move people forward. John Hagel brilliantly shows us how to use the power of a good narrative to get over the fears that hold too many individuals and business teams back and prevent them from achieving more impact. This thoughtfully rich book is sure to be essential reading for anyone trying to lead forward."

—**BETH COMSTOCK,** author of *Imagine It Forward* and former Vice Chair, General Electric

"Our mindsets are the most important tool we have as entrepreneurs and leaders, and they are powerfully shaped by the emotions within us. John Hagel's brilliant book *The Journey Beyond Fear* urges us to focus on our emotions and to recognize that fear is becoming a growing obstacle for many of us. Hagel masterfully guides us to shift our emotional energy into an Abundance Mindset, one that empowers us to solve problems and see them as opportunities rather than fear them."

—**PETER H. DIAMANDIS,** MD; Founder, Singularity University and XPRIZE, as well as *New York Times* bestselling author of *Abundance, BOLD,* and *The Future is Faster Than You Think*

"John Hagel has spent decades discovering new opportunities at the edges of organizations and markets. Drawing lessons from psychology, social movements, gaming platforms, innovative companies, and more, Hagel shows us how we can identify the passions that will motivate us to venture into new territory, overcome fear and self-limitations, and inspire others to join us in transforming institutions and society."

—**ROGER FERGUSON,** President and Chief Executive Officer of the Teachers Insurance and Annuity Association (TIAA) and former Vice Chairman of the Board of Governors of the Federal Reserve System

"John Hagel has done it again! From the depths and breath of his own experience, he gives us keys to a psychology that activates needed growth in self and society. This book is on the frontier of a conceptual evolution that brooks no whiney nay saying, but creates the ground for a dynamic transition into a Renaissance in thought and enterprise."

—**JEAN HOUSTON,** PhD, author of 30+ books in human development, Chancellor of Meridian University, and Chairman of the United Palace of Spiritual Arts in New York City

"It's easy to retreat with fear, but this timely book persuasively suggests there's another option: we can cultivate our excitement about exploration and learning to pursue the opportunities that are all around us. This book will help you realize far more of your potential and adapt to a rapidly changing world."

—**SCOTT BARRY KAUFMAN,** Professor of Psychology at Columbia University and author of many best-selling books on psychology, including *Transcend*

"Reading this thought-provoking book is like having John Hagel as our own personal executive coach, helping us move beyond our fears, craft a new personal narrative, and pursue the passions that enable us to have more positive impact. Part call to action, part cause for deep reflection, the book is one you'll be thinking about long after finishing the final chapter."

—**TOM KELLEY,** author of *Creative Confidence* and Partner in the design consultancy IDEO

"Fear can either paralyze you or propel you forward. This book shows you how to push through it, and serves as a reminder that it doesn't take big moves to make big impact."

—**ALISON LEVINE,** Team Captain, first American Women's Everest Expedition and author of *New York Times* bestseller *On the Edge*

"This is a must-read book for those who are seeking to increase their impact in the world around them. Sharing lessons from his own personal journey and broader research, John Hagel urges us to recognize the expanding opportunities that can be addressed once we find ways to overcome fear."

—**JOHN MACKEY,** Founder and CEO of Whole Foods Market and author of *Conscious Capitalism*

"*The Journey Beyond Fear* demonstrates that our success is more than strategic rationality—our passion and our fear are measurable, concrete determinants of life outcomes. Importantly, John moves beyond myths of 'you've got it or you don't' and presents an extensive vision for how to learn passion."

—**VIVIENNE MING,** theoretical neuroscientist, entrepreneur, and author; Co-Founder of Socos Labs, an independent institute exploring the future of human potential

"Fear is visceral but not sustainable. Joy, community, and love provide lasting motivation, passion, and success in all areas of life and are essential to our survival. In this brilliant book, John Hagel describes why, and how—which have never been more timely or needed."

—**DEAN ORNISH,** MD, Founder & President, Preventive Medicine Research Institute, Clinical Professor of Medicine, University of California, San Francisco, and author of *UnDo It!*

"John Hagel draws on his considerable experience and intellect to tackle a topic most organizations never confront: fear. With sharp insights and compelling cases, he shows how to move past fear to improve performance and deepen meaning. In a business world that often resists talking about emotions, this book is badly-needed guide to enlisting psychology in the service of your strategy."

—**DANIEL H. PINK,** author of *When*, *Drive*, and *To Sell Is Human*

"John Hagel sets himself a near-impossible task in offering to guide his readers 'beyond fear,' yet he delivers. The book pulls together many themes and insights that readers may think they already know, but will suddenly see in a new and useful light. Most important, Hagel's emphasis on the critical importance of 'learning platforms' is spot on, a dimension of how personal journeys can become collective journeys that is only beginning to be appreciated."

—**ANNE-MARIE SLAUGHTER,** CEO of New America, contributing editor of the *Financial Times,* and author of numerous bestselling books

THE
JOURNEY
BEYOND
FEAR

LEVERAGE THE THREE PILLARS
OF POSITIVITY
TO BUILD YOUR SUCCESS

JOHN HAGEL III

New York Chicago San Francisco Athens London Madrid
Mexico City Milan New Delhi Singapore Sydney Toronto

1 2 3 4 5 6 7 8 9   LCR   26 25 24 23 22 21

ISBN   978-1-264-26840-5
MHID   1-264-26840-8

e-ISBN   978-1-264-26841-2
e-MHID   1-264-26841-6

Library of Congress Cataloging-in-Publication Data

Names: Hagel, John, author.
Title: The journey beyond fear : leverage the three pillars of positivity to build
    your success / by John Hagel.
Description: 1 Edition. | New York City : McGraw Hill, 2021. |
    Includes bibliographical references and index.
Identifiers: LCCN 2021003122 (print) | LCCN 2021003123 (ebook) |
    ISBN 9781264268405 (hardback) | ISBN 9781264268412 (ebook)
Subjects: LCSH: Success in business. | Motivation (Psychology) |
    Leadership—Psychological aspects. | Fear.
Classification: LCC HF5386 .H2144 2021 (print) | LCC HF5386 (ebook) |
    DDC 658.4/09—dc23
LC record available at https://lccn.loc.gov/2021003122
LC ebook record available at https://lccn.loc.gov/2021003123

McGraw Hill books are available at special quantity discounts to use as premiums and sales promotions or for use in corporate training programs. To contact a representative, please visit the Contact Us pages at www.mhprofessional.com.

CONTENTS

PART 2
THE PASSION OF THE EXPLORER

PART 3
THE ROLE OF LEARNING
PLATFORMS

INTRODUCTION

As a child, I lived in a world of paradox. My globe-trotting father swept our family from Venezuela to Turkey and beyond, providing my sister and me with invaluable experiences. We learned multiple languages, were immersed in exotic cultures, and developed an inclusive, cosmopolitan perspective that was decades ahead of its time. But my childhood was far from perfect. I often felt alienated and lonely; worse still, my parents were deeply unhappy, and my sister and I bore the brunt of it.

As an adult, I live and work in a world that is no less paradoxical and troubling. A globalized marketplace and quantum leaps in computing power have speeded up the flow of knowledge and vastly improved productivity, but these same developments have shortened product cycles and heightened the competition for markets and jobs. Our world is filled with exhilarating opportunities but also with a debilitating pressure to perform, which leads to fear.

Opportunity and pressure, hope and fear—the tensions between these opposing forces shaped my life, sparking a passion that has sustained me for decades, connecting me with people from all walks of life who have helped me learn and grow. But they have also caused me no end of sorrow and struggle. All of us are living the same paradox, feeling on the one hand a sense of nearly limitless potential and on the other the fear of being left behind.

Our challenge is to respond to this pressure in ways that build hope and excitement, allowing us to seize the opportunities before us and make the most of them. Don't underestimate how difficult this is. Our instinctive responses to fear can easily erode, if not obliterate, those opportunities. Instead of grasping them and moving forward, we can just as easily withdraw, hiding from each other behind walls.

Think of your life as a journey by water. You start out with a vessel—yourself—that is more or less seaworthy, depending on your particular strengths and weaknesses. To reach your goal, you will need a powerful motivation (what I call a *narrative*) to impel you to set out from the safety of land; food and fuel to sustain you along the way (what I describe as *passion*); and perhaps most critically, help from others (via the learning *platforms* you can create to mobilize them). Narrative, passion, and platforms are the three pillars of positive emotion. Everyone's journey is unique, but we all need those three pillars if we are going to reach our destinations.

I'm in the midst of that journey myself, and whether you know it or not, you are too. Your career path is a part of it but by no means all of it. Your ultimate opportunity is to develop your own, your organization's, and ultimately all of humanity's potential in the fullest possible way.

In the pages that follow, I will tell you a lot more about narratives, passion, and platforms while sharing what I've learned on my own journey. This is not a memoir; my goal is to help you transform your own journey into one driven by hope and excitement rather than fear. But it is necessarily a personal book, because you can't fully tap your potential without confronting the emotions that stand in its way. Also, I'm going to resist citing the extensive literature and research that support my perspective. I know that will be frustrating to some readers (especially academics), but if I tried to include everything, the book would be at least twice as long as it is.

OPPORTUNITY AND PRESSURE

Both of my parents grew up in small towns, but they were driven to move beyond their comfort zones to explore and learn. My father, an executive at Mobil Oil, loved international assignments. My earliest memories are of a life filled to the brim with adventure as we moved from one far-flung place to another. I truly had marvelous opportunities, and I tried to make the most of them. Looking back, I am deeply grateful to my parents for providing me with them.

But there were challenges, too. As soon as I started to feel comfortable in a place, my father would announce a new assignment in a different country, and we would be uprooted. The next thing I knew, I'd be starting all over again in a new school. When I did make friends, I knew I'd have to leave them in a year or two when we moved again. All of this was before the internet and social media. Once we left, I'd quickly lose touch with my friends, no matter how close we'd become.

That would have been pressure enough. But my biggest challenges were on the home front. My mother, who'd survived a difficult childhood of her own, was filled with anger.

Like my father, she became the first in her family to attend college. She went on to earn her master's degree, intending to pursue a career with the State Department, which was quite an accomplishment in the 1940s. But then she sacrificed her ambitions for my father's. Frustrated, she lashed out at the daily challenges of life.

If you had met my mother outside the home, you would have found her to be warm and kind. At home, she was very different. One of my earliest memories is of her shouting that she wished I had never been born, that life would have been so much simpler and easier without me. Another very early memory is a tirade about how selfish and inconsiderate I was and how I should be focused on the needs of others, rather than my own. My mother never raised a hand to us, but she didn't have to. Her words were devastating enough.

My strong but gentle father loved her dearly, but her rage proved too much for him, and he gradually withdrew. His preferred escape was to his study and his stamp collection. As my sister and I became teenagers, he sought further escape in alcohol and pharmaceuticals—pain pills that numbed his ability to feel. He was not there for us when we needed him. No one was. Our extended family was back in the United States, so they couldn't see what was happening, never mind intervene.

Afraid of my mother's immense anger and desperate to win the kind of love I needed from my parents, I focused on getting top grades in school, since my parents respected academic achievement. That won me their praise, but I did not succeed in breaking through to the love I was seeking. Though I went on to earn multiple degrees and pursue a challenging career, it took me a long time and two failed marriages to realize I was on the wrong path.

I don't tell you all this to blame my parents. Looking back, I now realize they loved me deeply and in the best way they knew: they showed me the world and provided for all my material needs, including wonderful homes, extraordinary meals, and great schools. For that I am grateful, but they were not able to love me in the way I needed. My inability to receive that love shaped the path I pursued as a young person, a path that led to professional success but obscured what was meaningful to me.

OPPORTUNITY AND PRESSURE IN THE WORLD TODAY

Eventually, I landed in Silicon Valley, where I've lived for almost 40 years. Almost as soon as I arrived, the rapid and sustained improvements in digital technology that had begun there in the 1950s reached critical mass, unleashing a full-blown revolution.

Until then, powerful computers had been accessible to only the government and a few very large organizations that could afford mainframes. In the 1980s, they were becoming available to everyone. Today computing, storage, and networking technologies continue to advance at exponential rates, radically altering virtually every aspect of our lives. Biosynthesis technologies, 3D printing, and materials to build "smart" houses are transforming such diverse arenas as medicine, manufacturing, and construction. As with innovations throughout history, there is a significant lag between the introduction of new capabilities and the knowledge of how to harness them for good, but we're getting there. Thanks to wireless networks and drone technologies, for example, farmers in developing countries can connect with international markets, giving them better opportunities to sell at a fair price. And people with a wide variety of disabilities are benefiting from advances in implants and prosthetics. In some cases, these products also can augment the capabilities of healthy human bodies—for example, providing "exoskeletons" that can help warehouse workers move heavier objects without straining their muscles.

But here comes paradox again. All this opportunity has a dark side, which is gathering force at both the individual and institutional levels. As I discussed in my book *The Power of Pull*, these forces are reshaping our global economy and society. Digital-technology infrastructures are intensifying global competition. Customers can much more easily access vendors, regardless of where they are. New companies can find customers more quickly, wherever they are.

These digital-technology infrastructures are also increasing customer power. As consumers, we can quickly identify a broad range of vendors that might be available to address our needs, gather information about them and their products, and shift our business from one to another if our needs are not being met. Rather than settling for standardized mass-market products, we as customers are increasingly demanding products that meet our specific needs and tastes and that will evolve as they do. An early example of this is the rapid growth of craft beer and craft chocolates that address narrower and narrower segments of markets that large incumbents used to dominate with just a few offerings. Where once Americans would drink the same few pale lagers from a giant brewer and indulge a sweet tooth with milk chocolate from a giant candy company, today they might seek out a particular pumpkin stout or a fair-trade chocolate bar with 60 percent cacao.

The paradox arises because we are customers in one part of our lives but employees in another. The trends in globalization, technology, and customization are intensifying the pressure on our employers. The way employers harness these trends and meet the challenges often threatens jobs and consequently our livelihoods. The result of all this change is mounting pressure, for individuals and institutions alike.

The pressure on individuals was perfectly captured by a billboard I used to see beside Highway 101, which runs through the heart of Silicon Valley. The billboard asked a simple question: "How does it feel to know that there are at least 1 million people around the world who can do your job?" A few decades ago, the answer would have been obvious: It doesn't matter; I'm here and they're there. But now it does. More and more people are competing for our jobs, regardless of where they are on the planet. And in a world that is changing this fast, it matters less what our college degrees or professional certificates are or what we accomplished in the past. What matters is what we are learning *today* and, even more importantly, what we will learn tomorrow.

Besides competing with each other, we are competing with machines. Indeed, if that billboard came back today, it might read, "How does it feel to know that there are at least 1 million robots around the world who can do your job?" Automation is not just affecting low-skilled workers. Digital technology is carrying out tasks that used to be done by lawyers, journalists, and research scientists, and it's doing them faster, cheaper, and more accurately.

That's a lot of pressure at the individual level. But the pressure is also mounting for organizations. Many are slow to adapt and thus ripe for disruption. At Deloitte's Center for the Edge in Silicon Valley, the research center I founded and led for 13 years, we studied the long-term forces reshaping our global business landscape. We came to see that we were in the early stages of a Big Shift that has been transforming our global economy since the 1960s, when digital technology first became a significant factor in the business world.

We wanted to understand how companies were performing during this Big Shift. For our measure of financial performance, we selected return on assets (ROA), which essentially compares profits earned (reported on the income statement) with the assets required to support business activities (measured on the balance sheet). In our view, this was the best measure of the fundamental performance of a business. Many analysts look at returns to shareholders or return on equity, but the problem there is that many companies have found ways to manipulate these returns through financial engineering—for example, increasing dividend payments, increasing debt on the balance sheet, or buying back stock from shareholders. While this financial engineering can improve returns to shareholders in the short term, such returns are not sustainable. In contrast, ROA keeps the focus on the fundamental performance of the business.

When we looked at ROA for all public companies in the United States from 1965 to 2019, we saw something disconcerting. Over this period of more than five decades, ROA has declined by a whopping 75 percent. What's more, this long and sustained erosion shows no signs of leveling off, much less turning around.

When we first released these findings, some skeptics suggested that the erosion in performance might be concentrated in one or two industries. So we segmented all public companies into 13 different industries and found that the steep erosion was occurring in 11 of the 13 industries. The two exceptions were aerospace/defense and healthcare, and even there we found long-term erosion in performance, just not as severe as in the other industries.

While some companies performed better than others in all industries, their ability to sustain this superior performance was declining. The "topple rate" of companies falling out of the top quartile of performance was significantly increasing over time. This widespread and long-term erosion of financial performance is a striking indicator of mounting performance pressure. Twenty years ago, if you launched an amazing new product or service into the marketplace, you had a few years in which you could sit back, catch your breath, and in not a few cases, retire. Now if you launch an innovation, you immediately face a pair of questions: What do you have next? And how quickly can you get it to market?

We're not just in danger of losing our market share and our jobs; even our lives are at risk. Thanks to global connectivity, a small event in some faraway place can quickly cascade into an extreme event, whether it is a financial catastrophe, an act of terrorism, or the COVID-19 pandemic. It used to be that some core things in our world were constants we could rely on for support when we confronted unexpected situations. Those are few and far between today.

This growing pressure is intensified by an increasing disconnect between the way our institutions are run today and the way the world around them is changing. As we will see later in this book, our institutions will need to be fundamentally redesigned to overcome mounting pressure and target the expanding opportunities generated by the Big Shift.

HOW WE RESPOND TO MOUNTING PRESSURE AND ACCELERATING CHANGE

Human beings react to pressure and change in predictable ways. We tend to become risk averse, magnifying our perceptions of what can go wrong and discounting our perceptions of potential rewards. For instance, most of us are now comfortable with driving a car, but when something new, like autonomous vehicles, comes along, they sound terrifying to many people. That fear response takes the place of a side-by-side comparison of the risks and rewards of driving oneself versus using a self-driving car.

We also tend to shrink our time horizons, focusing more on the short term. With a mindset focused solely on the moment at hand, we believe that the rewards—or resources—available to us are strictly limited. The only question is who will get them—me or someone else. This drives us to adopt what economists call a *zero-sum* view of the world, in which for me to win, you have to lose. No win-win scenario is possible; there is no sharing of rewards. That mindset actively erodes trust. You may seem like a nice person, but at the end of the day, only one of us is going to get these resources, so I can't afford to trust you. It can easily create a vicious cycle in which we behave in ways that intensify rivalry, ratcheting up the pressure even more.

Pressure affects more than our cognitive biases and mindsets; we need to go one level deeper and explore its emotional impacts. During my travels around the world over the past several years, I have witnessed growing fear among people at every level of society. For example, when I spoke with senior executives in the privacy of their offices after taking the time to build some trust with them, I would inevitably discover that they felt enormous fear. They were acutely aware that the average tenure of a senior executive was significantly declining. Executives were getting removed if they missed their numbers by even a small amount. With accelerating change and growing uncertainty, they were afraid they would soon be out of their jobs. They might not have been willing to acknowledge that fear publicly, but the people around them could sense it.

Emotions have an interesting network effect: Once a critical mass of people feel a certain emotion, it tends to spread exponentially, both in terms of the number of people who feel it and in terms of the intensity with which it is felt. As the emotional cascade takes hold, it becomes harder and harder to resist.

Although I have worked as a business strategist for most of my career, I have come to believe that psychology is as important a factor in performance as strategy. If we don't understand the emotions driving our choices and actions, we'll never be able to get people to have more impact. A conversation with Dee Hock, the founder of Visa, brought this home to me. I was rambling on about the importance of risk and reward as motivators when he stopped me midsentence. "John," he said, "you've got it all wrong. It's not about risk and reward, it's about fear and hope. That's ultimately what motivates people to act."

My hope in writing this book is to help you become more aware of the emotion of fear and introduce you to the tools that can help you replace it with a sense of hope and excitement. As more and more of us do so, the same emotional network effect will take hold, only in a positive way. Of course, our fears can never disappear fully, but the key is to find the motivation to move forward in spite of them.

THE JOURNEY AHEAD

I felt deep fear as a child, but I tried to cope with it on multiple levels. First, I withdrew. When my mother erupted, I retreated to my bedroom and shut the door to block out as much as I could. Second, I used books. In particular, I escaped into science fiction, which allowed me to visit foreign worlds, not just the foreign countries we lived in. Happily, the science fiction from my childhood was generally optimistic, as it tended to show humans achieving unimaginable feats on a galactic scale.

This escape—actually a survival mechanism—turned out to be a healthy one, as it helped me cope with my fear and avoid the negative mindset that is a natural human reaction to pressure. It focused me on the amazing opportunities that would be available in the future and gave me confidence that our resources are not limited but capable of infinite expansion. And it convinced me that, by trusting each other and working together, we could accomplish awesome feats.

But reading science fiction couldn't fully protect me from the toxicity of my environment. My journey to recovery was not straightforward, and with the benefit of hindsight, I can see I could have pursued a different path that would have speeded up my healing and allowed me to transform the pressure I was feeling into opportunity. That is the path I'm going to tell you about in this book.

As I mentioned earlier, to succeed in your journey, you will need three essential tools: narratives, passion, and platforms—the three pillars of positive emotion. As you will see, I define them in a very particular way:

- Narratives are the *catalysts* that help you see the need for a journey. From my perspective, they are about something in the future that has not yet been achieved, and they provide an explicit call to action.

- Passion is the *fuel* that moves you ahead, helping you overcome the inevitable roadblocks and obstacles you will inevitably confront along the way. The specific form of passion I will be exploring involves a commitment to making an increasing impact in a domain that excites you.

- Platforms are how you connect with other people on similar journeys. They are *accelerants* that help you to move more quickly and achieve more impact. Platforms explicitly designed to help participants connect and learn faster together are particularly powerful.

In a digitally connected, globalized world, people and companies need to learn how to find and tap people and resources wherever they find them—something I've called the power of pull. The highest level of pull is the ability to draw out more of our own potential from within ourselves. If we look deep within ourselves, we all have a strong need and desire to achieve more of our potential and to help our loved ones achieve more of their potential as well.

We can achieve more of our potential when we find ways to build relationships with others. Narratives, passion, and platforms are key enablers of that highest level of pull. In fact, the ultimate goal of our journey is not what we can do for ourselves, but for our personal transformations to lead to the transformation of the institutions and the broader society they are embedded in, which grew out of a very different set of opportunities and constraints than the ones that define our world today. The results from our analysis of US public companies' return on assets are just one indication of the growing disconnect between the institutions we have today and the institutions we will need to create to address our expanding opportunities.

Our large institutions today—companies, governments, schools, and nonprofits—are organized around models of scalable efficiency, in which work consists of tightly specified and highly standardized routine tasks. These institutions are risk averse and discourage anyone from improvising or deviating from their assigned tasks. They tend to feed the fear of their participants, suggesting that participants are at increasing risk of losing their jobs if they fail to deliver as expected.

While we need to begin with ourselves in the journey beyond fear, we also will need to reach out and connect with others to find ways to drive the broader changes we need. If we focus only on ourselves, our institutions and broader society will hold us back. Conversely, if we focus on changing our institutions and broader society without addressing our own emotions and behaviors, we won't get very far at all.

For decades now, a robust and growing human potential movement has sought to help us thrive as individuals. Numerous movements for institutional and social change also are working to create environments that will be more supportive of people. But these movements rarely interact with each other, much less integrate their agendas for change. We need to bring them together so they can drive sustainable and scalable change across the board.

This is not just an opportunity. It's an imperative. The seas we are navigating are becoming more and more turbulent. It is no exaggeration to say that our future is hanging in the balance. We could be sailing toward a future whose wonders would amaze even the science fiction writers I read as a child—or we could founder along the way.

As we make this journey, we will inevitably confront some core questions:

- How can I move beyond fear and find ways to cultivate hope and excitement?

- How can I connect with others to make this journey together?

- How can we amplify our impact in the areas that really excite us?

My goal in writing this book is to bring us together to answer these questions, so we can start to build a world driven by hope and excitement rather than fear.

PART 1

THE ROLE OF OPPORTUNITY-BASED NARRATIVES

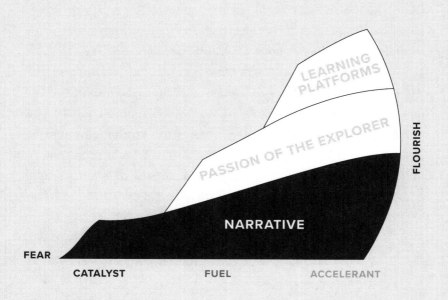

This book has three parts, one for each of the pillars of positive emotion. In the first, we will explore narratives and how they can become a powerful catalyst to help us move beyond fear. I use the word *narrative* to mean something different from what most people think of when they hear it, so I will begin by clarifying the term and explaining why narrative in the sense I describe can be so powerful.

The rest of this part focuses on specific levels of narratives. Chapter 2 is about our personal narratives, which provide us with motivation to act. Chapter 3 discusses institutional narratives—the narratives that all institutions have and that represent a call to action they issue to their stakeholders and customers. Chapter 4 ventures up to a higher level and investigates geographical narratives. Chapter 5 looks at the role that movement-based narratives have played in mobilizing people to come together to achieve significant change. Finally, in Chapter 6, I make the case that we will be most successful in overcoming fear and achieving impact when our narratives at every level are aligned.

CHAPTER 1

THE POWER OF NARRATIVE

*How It Pulls People to Act,
Innovate, and Learn*

Everyone talks about the importance of story and narrative. Big brands and their marketers do. So do politicians. But they use the terms *story* and *narrative* loosely and usually interchangeably, as if they have the same meaning. I make a critical distinction between those two words—one that plays a key role in our journey from fear and pressure to opportunity and unleashed potential.

THE DISTINCTION BETWEEN STORIES AND NARRATIVES

Stories have two key attributes. First, they are self-contained. As Aristotle observed, they have a beginning, a middle, and most importantly, an end. For all their twists and turns, they resolve.

The second attribute of the stories we read (or hear or watch) is that they are not specifically about us. They can be about the storyteller. They can be about other people (or made-up characters if they are fiction), but they are not about us. We can use our imagination to place ourselves in them vicariously, imagining how it might feel to be one of their characters, but in the end, stories are about other people.

Stories are powerful because they excite our imaginations and draw out deep emotions. They can teach us in nonthreatening ways by immersing us in situations that create and resolve conflict and open up new worlds. They can provide us with deep insights into how to respond to particular challenges and opportunities. Their greatest value is that they move beyond our minds to tap into the emotions and spirit that ultimately shape our views of the world and the actions we take in it.

Narratives differ significantly on these two attributes. First, they are open ended. There is no resolution, at least not yet. Some significant opportunity or threat exists in the future, but it has not yet been determined whether the opportunity will be successfully addressed or whether the threat will be overcome. Second, the narrative is about *us*. It is a personal call to action, because its outcome depends upon what we do. We are not just passive observers but active participants in it.

To be clear, some narratives do resolve, but the resolution is out in the future, and the nature of the resolution is uncertain. It will depend upon the actions taken (or not taken) by those who are called to act. Suppose a narrative is focused on a potential threat: an invasion by an enemy country. That threat may become a reality if we choose not to act, it may be averted if we build strong enough defenses, or it may continue to exist indefinitely, requiring us to remain constantly vigilant.

Companies may seek to motivate action from their customers by calling attention to a big threat they face. A healthcare company might focus customers' attention on life-threatening diseases and seek to motivate action through their fear of death. A better, more powerful type of narrative is opportunity based. Opportunity-based narratives focus instead on the ability to achieve a positive impact for yourself or for those you care about by doing something previously thought impossible. These opportunities can take many different forms. They may be business opportunities, in the sense that they generate and capture significant economic value. They may be personal opportunities, like the ability to help children grow and develop in richer ways. Or they could be social opportunities, like the ability to foster communities whose members are committed to helping each other in times of need. Whatever their context, the key is that they identify opportunities that can inspire and excite people in ways that will help them to move beyond fear and achieve more meaningful impact.

High-impact, opportunity-based narratives should focus on opportunities that will not be resolved for a significant period of time, so they can motivate and mobilize large numbers of people. One example is the opportunity to ensure that everyone in the world has access to potable water. If all the right people mobilize and work together toward its fulfillment, we may someday fully realize this opportunity, and the narrative will come to an end (at which point it will become a story). Of course, there could be progress along the way.

Someone could find a creative approach that delivers water to certain villages in Bangladesh. This could then inspire local entrepreneurs to do the same for other villages, in even more cost-effective ways. The broader opportunity—bringing high-quality water to everyone—would still be unresolved, but we could now tell a story about how success was achieved in Bangladesh and use it to inspire others to take action in other parts of the world.

Threat-based narratives can be reframed as opportunity-based narratives. Take the example of the healthcare company. Rather than focusing on the danger of life-threatening diseases, the company might focus on our opportunity to live healthier lives. This could inspire us to take broader and more sustained actions to cultivate our well-being, ultimately reducing our risk—and our fear—of disease.

Some opportunities are unlikely to ever be fully realized but are noble and irresistible quests, so they provide the foundation for enduring narratives. Take the example of a narrative that focuses on the opportunity to achieve more of our potential. If you believe, as I do, that our potential as humans is limitless, then this narrative will continue to unfold indefinitely.

Narratives have played major roles throughout history. Every major religion is driven by an opportunity-based narrative. Christianity, for example, teaches that we are born in sin, but a savior came to earth to redeem us. Salvation is not guaranteed; we must first accept that savior and live by his teachings. Buddhism doesn't involve a personal savior but offers a path to happiness through meditation and renunciation. Islam requires its followers to surrender to the will of Allah. Salvation, nirvana, and surrender are never fully achieved; their pursuit becomes a way of life. Beyond one's personal redemption, religions offer their followers opportunities to help others by encouraging them to make the right choices. As such, they become the bases of communities.

Successful political movements are driven by narratives as well. The Marxist narrative, for example, has had tremendous impact in many parts of the world. It offers an opportunity to build a fair society in which everyone prospers. But first, workers must mobilize to overthrow capitalism. Their actions determine how the narrative will resolve.

Stories are effective because they engage us emotionally. I would argue that narratives have even more power. Throughout history, they have motivated millions of people to work and struggle against seemingly impossible odds and even to make the ultimate sacrifice. Consider the Christian martyrs or the Bolsheviks who died in the Russian Revolution, driven by the opportunity to build a socialist society. Or look at the early Jewish settlers in modern Israel, who were willing to fight and die for their promised land. The willingness to make that ultimate sacrifice is a power that few, if any, stories can inspire. What makes narratives so powerful is their explicit call to action—the message that their successful resolution depends upon what we do.

I'm not suggesting that narratives should replace stories. Narratives and stories reinforce each other in powerful ways. The story about bringing water to those villages in Bangladesh strengthens the credibility of the larger narrative about bringing water to the whole world. Individuals and companies will be more motivated to join the effort when they see that others are making progress. On the other side of the coin, a story gains more power if it can be positioned in the context of a broader narrative. What happened in Bangladesh was not just a one-off event but part of something much bigger: the yet-to-be-achieved opportunity to bring water to everyone. Narratives describe the journey and why it's worth the effort, while stories help us to understand the steps along the way and the impact that can be achieved.

Here's a business example. A car company crafts a narrative urging us to broaden our horizons by exploring the world, venturing into areas we have never visited. The narrative might suggest that the opportunity is to discover our passion in unexpected areas. The company then reinforces that narrative by telling stories of people who explored new areas and made discoveries that ignited a long-term passion.

Narratives without stories are too abstract, and stories without narratives can have limited impact. When I was growing up, stories were extremely important to me, but they only provided me with a temporary escape. They inspired me with hope, but they didn't provide me with a sense of agency—a call to action that could change my life—because they were about other people. I needed a narrative that would motivate me to improve not only my own life but also the lives of others, inspiring them to join me in the same quest. It wasn't until many years later that I found it.

In a world of mounting pressure, we have a natural tendency to become passive. Overwhelmed, we begin to lose the hope that we can make a difference. The power of narrative is that it moves us from observers to active participants. It helps persuade us that what we do matters.

Narratives help us overcome our fear-driven passivity by giving us a sense of a future that is worth striving for today. By focusing us on an inspiring opportunity, they help us avoid the risk of simply becoming reactive to whatever is going on at the moment and spreading ourselves too thinly across too many fronts.

Narratives also provide stability, and in a world of accelerating change and uncertainty, this is critical. We become disoriented and anxious when we lack something to hold onto. Perhaps this is why one of the most significant global trends over the past 50 years has been the growth of fundamentalist religions, which emphasize rules, precepts, and codes of behavior that never change.

Narratives don't have to last an eternity (although some do have that potential). But they must pull us out of the present and persuade us that something significant lies ahead, providing us with a North Star that gives us a long-term objective, rather than an anchor that holds us back. In short, narratives have the power to do four things:

- **Focus us on the future.** Narratives help us overcome our natural tendency to hide away when we are consumed by fear. By defining some compelling opportunity or threat in the future, they help us look ahead, motivating us to invest the time and effort necessary to achieve something that has not yet been achieved.

- **Focus us on action.** Narratives point to actions we can take today to address the longer-term opportunity or threat, helping us to overcome the passivity that often grips us when we are driven by fear. Action then drives a powerful form of learning that is different from what we can learn by listening to a story. When we learn through action, we gain insights into what kinds of actions have the greatest impact, allowing us to evolve them in real time.

- **Focus us on others.** Narratives help us overcome our fear-driven sense of isolation. They bring us together, so we can amplify our impact and learn even faster than we could on our own. The shared commitment helps build trust and a sense of deep connection that motivates us to take even bolder actions.

- **Catalyze passion.** As I'll develop further in later chapters, narratives can be catalysts for a specific form of passion, the passion of the explorer. This passion shifts our reaction to unexpected challenges from fear to hope and excitement, motivating us to overcome whatever obstacles we might encounter in pursuit of our long-term goals.

DIFFERENT LEVELS OF NARRATIVES

Narratives can be defined and pursued on multiple levels: personal, institutional, geographical, and movement based. Chapters 2 through 5 will explore each of these in greater depth, but here's an overview:

- **Personal narratives.** Although the term *personal narratives* may sound like stories about you, these narratives actually are designed to help you gain support from others. Instead of explaining what you have done in the past, they describe what you want to accomplish in the future, why others would want to join you, and what would motivate them to make that effort.

- **Institutional narratives.** At the institutional level, narratives connect people who do not work for the institution with opportunities related to the institution's mission. A bank might have a narrative that focuses on what we must do to ensure that our children lead even more fulfilling lives than we have. If people respond by doing more long-term financial planning, the bank could attract new customers, increase the loyalty of its current customers, and potentially expand the array of services it offers them. But the call action is not "subscribe to more of our services." The narrative should reveal a deep understanding of what the customer needs, inspiring them to seek it out themselves.

- **Geographical narratives.** Powerful narratives have emerged around cities, regions, and even countries, contributing to their success at different points in history. These geographical narratives draw people to a place and align them so they can achieve something meaningful. At the turn of the last century, Vienna had such a narrative, which was about the opportunity to move beyond the narrow focus on reason in the Enlightenment and to explore the complex motivations that shape human behavior to develop a much deeper understanding of what it means to be human. This made Vienna a magnet for talent in many different disciplines. Today Silicon Valley has a narrative about the opportunity to change the world with digital technology.

- **Movement-based narratives.** Religious, political, and economic movements utilize narratives to address a significant opportunity or threat. For example, the abolitionist movement in the 19th century brought people around the world together to seek the emancipation of slaves. Movement-based narratives are largely independent of geography or seek significant change within a geography, as in the case of a liberation movement in a country ruled by a dictator.

Narratives have the greatest impact when, at a minimum, the first three levels are aligned. In contrast, if our personal narrative is not effectively aligned with the narratives of our institutional and geographical settings, we will grow frustrated and find it difficult to seize the opportunities we desire.

The story of my life has in large part been an effort to align my evolving personal narrative with both an institutional and a geographical narrative. At one point, I began to evolve a personal narrative of venturing out beyond well-established areas and exploring emerging "edges," but at the time, I was involved in institutions that were risk averse and had narratives that encouraged people to follow well-established paths. My personal narrative didn't achieve real impact until I ventured out to institutions and places that embraced the desire to explore the edge.

I should pause here to explain what I mean by "edge," since I will be using this term frequently. *Edges* are areas that provide rich opportunities for learning in the form of the creation of new knowledge. Edges can be new domains, like new waves of technology, new generations of people coming into our economy and society, or economies around the world that are rapidly developing. Edges can also be the boundaries between existing domains, like the borders between two very different communities or the walls that separate academic disciplines, like economics and history. When we venture out onto edges, we are likely to move beyond our comfort zone, but we are also likely to learn a lot faster than if we remained in the areas we already know well.

OPPORTUNITY-BASED NARRATIVES HAVE MORE POTENTIAL THAN THREAT-BASED NARRATIVES

As noted earlier in this chapter, narratives may be either opportunity based or threat based. Which type of narrative you choose to pursue will have a significant impact on your mindset, emotions, and actions.

Threat-based narratives—those that tell you a significant threat is approaching—tend to reinforce a negative mindset and a feeling of fear. Threat-based narratives magnify our perception of risk, shorten our time horizons, cause us to fall into a zero-sum view of the world, and make it difficult for us to trust others. In sum, they exaggerate the perception of pressure and amplify all the natural human reactions we have to it. They move us to act but in very narrow and often unproductive ways.

The political environment in the United States is increasingly driven by threat-based narratives. We're under attack, the enemy is coming to get us, we're all about to die (or at least lose everything we hold dear) unless we move quickly to fight the enemy. The enemy differs, of course, depending on your political beliefs, but the message from both sides of the aisle is clear: we are in imminent danger. Is it any wonder that these threat-based narratives feed our fear, accelerate our loss of trust, and shrink our time horizons?

Opportunity-based narratives, in contrast, help us overcome our natural human reactions to threats and fear. Think of the "I Have a Dream" speech that Martin Luther King Jr. delivered at the Lincoln Memorial in 1963, during the March on Washington for Jobs. What made his speech so inspiring was the opportunity it described for all of us to come together and live as equals.

Because opportunity-based narratives move us to act in positive ways—to seize a future opportunity—they help minimize our feelings of fear and strengthen our feelings of hope and excitement. Opportunities in this kind of narrative tend to be ones that can be more easily achieved if others join the quest, and they expand with the number of participants. So we are no longer dealing with a zero-sum view of the world with a fixed set of resources, but with a positive-sum view of a world in which new resources can always be found and opportunities are continually expanding.

By highlighting the potential rewards available to the many, opportunity-based narratives encourage us to collaborate, leveraging each other's capabilities so we can move faster and with greater impact than if we were acting alone. As we shift to a positive-sum view of the world, we become more willing to trust others.

One especially beneficial aspect of opportunity-based narratives is that they can pull in people we might never have met otherwise. Such serendipitous encounters can be hugely valuable in your journey. Some historians have suggested that the origin of the modern feminist movement in the United

States was the serendipitous encounters between women who were drawn into the civil rights movement, who then hatched the idea of a similar movement dedicated to creating more opportunities for women.

As we will see later in the book, the Silicon Valley narrative has inspired people from all over the world to come to Silicon Valley to start businesses that leverage digital technology. One of the keys to its success is the serendipitous encounters that occur in meeting rooms and social gatherings, connecting people who otherwise would have never met. The conversations that result from these encounters often generate new ideas and approaches to the challenges entrepreneurs confront as they seek to bring new technologies to market. As one example, Sergei Brin was the student who took Larry Page on the tour of the Stanford campus when Larry was applying to graduate school there. This chance meeting led the two founders of Google to connect and come up with an idea for a company to help people more readily access the vast array of information being made available on the internet.

Opportunity-based narratives also accelerate learning and drive innovation. Look back at John F. Kennedy's inspirational challenge to Congress and the nation in 1961 to come together around the opportunity to land a man on the moon within the decade. The unprecedented opportunity he framed brought many groups of scientists and engineers together, not just at NASA but also at universities and scientific institutions around the country.

More recently, an entrepreneur named Peter Diamandis created an opportunity-based narrative about the commercial potential of space travel. He made the opportunity much more tangible by offering a $10 million prize to the first privately financed team to build and fly a three-passenger vehicle 100 kilometers into space twice within a period of two weeks. The resulting contest motivated 26 teams from seven nations to invest more than $100 million. Eight years later, an entrepreneurial team won that prize. But the opportunity framed by the narrative was much bigger than that one prize and helped to catalyze a new multibillion-dollar industry.

As their number expands, the participants in a narrative tend to cluster into small groups and try different approaches to achieving the opportunity. Everyone gets to observe the impact of these approaches and integrate aspects of the successful ones into their own activities. By moving in parallel and continuously reflecting on what they—and others—have done, they learn much faster than any one person could on his or her own. Opportunity-based narratives thus harness the power of "pull": they pull out more of the participants' potential by accelerating learning.

I need to stress something here. The distinction between threat- and opportunity-based narratives is not black and white; the reality is more complex. Narratives that are primarily focused on a future threat may also make some reference to the opportunity that awaits if the threat is defeated. However, those narratives focus more on the threat because the consequences of failure are so severe. Opportunity-based narratives likewise acknowledge the challenges and obstacles. In fact, an awareness of challenges and obstacles is essential for these narratives to succeed. If there is no challenge or problem to solve, the narrative will be less likely to motivate people to act. As Kennedy said in his moonshot speech, we choose to accept the challenge not because the things we will have to do "are easy, but because they are hard."

WHAT ABOUT METANARRATIVES OR "GRAND NARRATIVES"?

You may also have heard of another kind of narrative, called a metanarrative or "grand narrative." These are a popular topic in the academic world. While definitions vary, metanarratives or grand narratives typically offer a comprehensive explanation of how the world works. For example, the grand narrative of the Enlightenment was that rational thought and science would inevitably improve the human condition.

Today, many grand narratives compete for our attention. The globalist grand narrative says that the more connected the world becomes, the greater the prosperity for everyone. The urbanist grand narrative declares that more and more people will come together in ever larger and more prosperous cities, and that those who don't will be left behind.

Grand narratives are very different from the kinds of narratives I describe, as they tell us how the world inevitably works. Because of this, they tend to foster passivity. Whether for good or ill, this is how things are, they say. We can't change that; we can only accept it and act accordingly.

WHAT ABOUT VIDEO GAMES AND VIRTUAL REALITY?

Many of my techie friends have pushed back on the distinction I make between stories and narratives. They point out that video games and, more recently, virtual-reality platforms are not self-contained. That's true. Although some video games have an end and declare winners (and losers), others can be played endlessly with ever-increasing levels of challenge and reward. *World of Warcraft* is one of the best-known examples of an endless video game. Drawing us into an incredibly complex virtual world that involves warring groups on fantasy planets, it offers us the opportunity to shape the outcome of the battles that will determine who ultimately wins the war. We are most definitely not just passive observers.

The rise of simulated-reality platforms takes it to another level. With those, we are drawn into environments where, unlike video games, few rules or even guidelines define the actions we can take. Take the example of *Minecraft*, which has amassed over 126 million active players worldwide. There's the challenge of staying alive in dangerous environments, but the real attraction of *Minecraft* is the opportunity to collaborate on creating awesome structures, including forts, schools, and supermarkets. We explore and create the environment, rather than just passively observe it.

While these games and platforms don't meet my criteria for stories, they aren't narratives either. They might inspire action in the real world, but that isn't their primary objective. Their goal is to draw us out of our current environment to explore some imaginary worlds. This will be even more true as virtual-reality experiences become more broadly available. A true narrative provides a call to action now and in the real world. Perhaps we could classify video games and simulated-reality platforms as "virtual narratives"? This would acknowledge that they are different from stories and don't meet the criteria for true narratives. But it doesn't allay my concern that these virtual narratives can foster passivity in the real world. By providing us with such rich alternative realities, they can motivate us to withdraw from reality.

Of course, technology will continue to challenge the classic boundaries between reality and virtual reality. I'm particularly intrigued by the potential of the augmented-reality platforms that overlay virtual elements onto the world we interact with daily. The global craze for *Pokémon Go* in 2016, in which players attempted to "catch" the virtual creatures on street corners, restaurants, and in their own bedrooms, suggests how popular they may become. Games like that certainly motivate us to venture out into the real world in search of opportunities. But again, the opportunities are virtual rather than real. We are not motivated to change the world, but simply to use it as the context for an imaginary quest. This could, and likely will, change over time. We already have early augmented-reality tools that can be used by workers to get more information and insight about their environments. For example, there are headsets for surgeons that provide real-time information about their patients.

I can imagine a growing range of simulated-reality, virtual-reality, and augmented-reality platforms that will help participants seeking to address longer-term threats or opportunities in the real world. It's not hard for me to imagine a narrative crafted around the opportunity to "grow" human organs in the laboratory so we no longer have to rely on donated ones. Augmented-reality devices could be very helpful in assessing the viability of organs and could help surgeons transplanting them. But such devices would be tools that support a narrative, much as online discussion forums and search tools do today, rather than representing the narrative itself.

WHAT MAKES A STRONG OPPORTUNITY-BASED NARRATIVE?

From this point on, I will focus exclusively on opportunity-based narratives; I will only mention threat-based narratives to highlight how they differ from those that focus on a big opportunity in the future.

Through working with dozens of individuals and companies to craft their narratives and crafting my own, I have found that the most powerful opportunity-based narratives have the following qualities:

- **The narrative is aligned with broader forces shaping the global landscape.** If the opportunity you have framed does not align with current social and economic trends, no amount of effort will help you accomplish it. An opportunity needs to be achievable. If the forces of the world are conspiring against it, you will have a hard time mobilizing and sustaining the support you need. For example, if your narrative focuses on the opportunity to shift from fossil fuels to alternative energy sources, it will be aligned with the broader technology trends that make it feasible. If you believe the opportunity is to return to wood-burning fires as our primary source of energy, that narrative is not likely to get much traction.

- **The narrative invites open-ended participation.** Powerful narratives frame opportunities for action and impact at a very high level but leave enough room for individuals or small groups to be creative. By remaining at a high level, they can evolve to accommodate changing circumstances (and will have to, since the opportunity framed by the narrative is likely to take a long time to achieve). Framing the opportunity as the development of alternative energy sources needn't lock a company or person into a specific source, nor must it specify the technology that will be required to harness its full economic potential.

• **The narrative defines the opportunity with enough detail and context to motivate and focus participants.** To justify a significant effort by participants, the opportunity needs to be credible (although not inevitable); it must have enough detail and context to ensure that participants will operate in complementary and reinforcing ways, rather than fragmenting into less effective camps. For example, various movements seeking to promote "social justice" have floundered because the opportunity is so broad and subject to so many interpretations that it has been difficult to mobilize enough people in a sustained way. Movements seeking to promote the rights of specific ethnic groups or women have had much more impact.

• **The narrative defines an opportunity that appeals to many participants.** If the opportunity affects only a small group of people, it will likely have far less impact than one with a much broader appeal. Of course, context matters here. If this is a personal narrative or a narrative for a small community, the number of people drawn to the narrative may matter less than if it is a narrative for a large institution, country, or movement.

- **The opportunity amplifies other opportunities.** A challenging but important principle is that, wherever possible, it is helpful to show how the opportunity that is the focus of a narrative connects with and amplifies other opportunities. If your personal narrative is focused on the opportunity to cultivate awe-inspiring gardens, it would be helpful to explore how this opportunity could support other opportunities that excite others, like helping marginalized people find productive work or helping to capture carbon from the atmosphere. This will help bring others into your cause, even if it's only a small subset of people.

- **The narrative defines an opportunity with deep emotional appeal.** A good narrative shouldn't be simply rationally attractive. It must tap into people's hopes, aspirations, and excitement to sustain them on their quests, given how many challenges and obstacles they are likely to meet. Remember the previous example of a bank whose institutional narrative is helping our children lead more fulfilling lives. If that narrative had been framed in purely financial terms, it would have had far less impact.

- **The narrative is realistic about challenges and obstacles**. A strong narrative excites people about the opportunity while also alerting them to the risks. Yes, there's a fine line here. You want to avoid threat-based narratives. But the message needs to be that the opportunity is not a given or predetermined. Achieving it will take effort, because the obstacles and roadblocks standing in the way of its completion are not trivial and cannot all be predicted.

- **The narrative presents positive-sum opportunities.** A strong narrative creates incentives for many people to come together to address the opportunity. If we're in a zero-sum world, where either you win or I win, it is much more difficult for us to collaborate. In contrast, if we're in a positive-sum world, where we expand the rewards by working together, we are much more motivated to collaborate with each other—and to invite still more people to work with us.

- **The narrative provides tangible and relatively quick benefits to early participants.** Powerful narratives reduce barriers to entry by delivering results to early participants, without requiring them to invest a significant amount of time and effort. For example, a narrative that focuses on the opportunity to develop alternative energy sources can focus on deploying some of the viable technologies that already exist, even though there is a long way to go before they can fully replace fossil fuels.

HOW DO YOU CRAFT A POWERFUL OPPORTUNITY-BASED NARRATIVE?

As we will explore in more detail in the chapters ahead, narratives are not words on a page. You can't create a narrative just by writing it down. Narratives emerge from action—action that is sustained over time. They can start with inspiration, with individuals or groups acquiring some sense that a significant opportunity exists—for example, for the clients of a bank to help their children to lead more fulfilling lives—but these narratives take shape and evolve through action.

Action is also key to both credibility and learning. If we're not taking action to help our children lead more fulfilling lives, we'll never really understand what actions have the greatest impact. If an individual or small group sees an opportunity and does nothing beyond writing it down, they will be far less credible when inviting participants to join that narrative. They would be more successful if they put their words into action. If the key executives of that bank are not helping their own children lead more fulfilling lives, no amount of marketing is going build trust and credibility in the narrative. When participants take action, they sharpen their view of the opportunity and generate insight into how they can most quickly seize it. As others join in, the learning expands.

It is often helpful to step back and articulate the narratives, whether they were conscious or not, that got you to the point where you are today. In doing so, you may find that your call to action focuses on an opportunity that is not the most meaningful to potential participants or that it is not framed in a way that can really motivate them. By looking at the impact (or lack of it) you've achieved in the past, you may discover opportunities to achieve far more.

You might also benefit from reflecting on the ways you have participated in other people's narratives in the past. Was the opportunity they were framing truly meaningful to you? Perhaps you should embrace someone else's opportunity as your own or work to help them reframe their narrative so they can achieve even more impact. You might also reflect on whether the actions you are taking are the most impactful ones you could be doing. These reflections could be helpful for a broad range of narratives that are relevant to you: your personal narrative, an institutional narrative, and the broader geographical and movement-based narratives you are contributing to.

Here's a piece of good news: we now have at our disposal an increasingly powerful set of digital technologies that can help us assess the impact of our existing narratives while simultaneously drawing more people to join us. To understand what marvelous tools digital technologies are, think of the great narratives of the past. To penetrate society, they had to transcend the confines of their existing communications media. Major religions often relied on core texts at the outset, and of course, proponents of the religions could spread the word through inspiring speeches. Then they evolved their approaches as the available media did: they moved into art, music, theater, and later radio, film, and video to spread the narrative. But that was just the beginning. The most successful religious leaders and teachers today leverage the full range of new technologies, like social media and instant messaging.

Moving to a business setting, imagine the resources a healthcare company could harness to communicate a narrative around the opportunity to improve consumers' wellness. It could use printed texts and videos to provide an initial call to action, but that's just the beginning. It could convene small groups of people interested in wellness to meet on a regular basis. These groups could then connect into larger online communities.

Digital technology allows anyone to define and communicate their narratives in rich and textured ways that supplement conventional text-based forms of communication. These methods often have much greater reach. As one example, look at the success of "Kid President" (Robby Novak), who when he was 11 years old did a YouTube video in which he shared an inspiring narrative about the opportunity for all of us to come together to create something that will make the world an amazing place. The video went viral and reached more than 30 million views. Certainly, Black Lives Matter and other contemporary political movements have found ways to engage a larger number of people by using social media and online platforms. We have the tools; we need to put them to good use as powerful new narratives emerge.

Finally, let me be clear that narratives themselves are tools. When I talk about the power of narrative, I am talking about its power as a tool. It is up to us to use them in ways that unleash that power.

BOTTOM LINE

Narratives are a powerful tool to help us on our journey beyond fear, but they must be understood and applied in a very specific way.

- **Narratives are very different from stories: they are open ended, without a resolution, and have an explicit call to take action to make a resolution possible.**

- **Narratives that focus on opportunities in the future have the greatest potential to help us overcome our fear and motivate us to take action. Threat-based narratives tend to feed the fear and should be avoided if our intent is to move beyond fear.**

- **Narratives are not just words on a page. They emerge and evolve through action. The most effective narratives bring people together to pursue action together.**

- **Narratives can be developed at multiple levels, explored in more detail in Chapters 2 through 6.**

- **Strong opportunity-based narratives have certain characteristics that can be helpful to understand as we craft our own narratives.**

CHAPTER 2

PERSONAL NARRATIVES

Overcoming Isolation

Fear is a natural reaction to the mounting performance pressure that increasingly characterizes our world, and it has predictable consequences. It magnifies our perception of risk, shrinks our time horizons, and causes us to fall prey to a zero-sum view of the world that leads us to distrust others. Inevitably, we find it harder to build deep and enduring relationships, and we become more and more isolated. The more isolated we become, the more pressure we experience. As the pressure mounts, the feeling of isolation intensifies, adding to our sense of helplessness and fear.

How can we break out of this vicious cycle? As with all emotions, the answer begins with us as individuals. We need to look within and reflect on our view of the future and the roles we are asking others to play in it. In other words, we need to reflect on the personal narrative shaping our choices and actions.

IT'S NOT JUST ABOUT YOU

Despite the descriptive term "personal," your narratives are ultimately not just about you, but about the call to action you issue to others you are trying to reach and motivate. This use of narrative is quite different from the large and robust school of human psychology that focuses on the concept of "personal narrative." Their view of personal narrative, to put it as simply as possible, is more in line with what Chapter 1 describes as stories. From this psychological standpoint, a personal narrative is an individual's construction of the story of their life. It's used in therapy to look backward, exploring the past to gain insight into why you have lived your life the way you have. Such an exercise certainly can be valuable.

The kinds of personal narratives that I describe emphasize the future, rather than the past. They are about your perception of a big opportunity or threat in the future—one that can shape your choices and actions. Your view of your past will influence your choices and actions, but your view of the future will have a greater impact on how you will act.

There's another difference. Psychological narratives tend to focus on individuals and how they have lived their lives. What I call a personal narrative is really about your call to action to others—what you want other people to do to help you address the future opportunity or threat you see. This connects you with others in ways that pull you and them out of fear-induced isolation, providing mutual benefit.

Few of us have given much thought to how we would articulate our personal narrative, let alone reflected upon whether doing so can truly help us achieve more of our potential. I didn't do that until fairly late in my life, and it changed my whole trajectory. Looking into our past can give us insights into how we evolved our current narrative and whether it has achieved the impact we desired. But the focus ultimately needs to be on our view of the future and the role we want those around us to play in it.

CRAFTING YOUR
PERSONAL NARRATIVE

To help you to think about your personal narrative and how you might craft one, I'm going to share the evolution of my personal narrative. When I did finally sit down to reflect on it, I began by focusing on my life as a child and young adult. The chief lesson I took from my family experience was that my own emotional needs were irrelevant. My mother had clearly communicated to me that life is challenging for everyone and that my role was to try to be aware of the needs of others (especially hers) and serve them as best I could.

That provided the foundation for the threat-based narrative that shaped my choices and actions through much of my early adulthood. Of course, I never put it into words, but if I had, it would have gone something like this: "Our world is full of challenges. Tell me the ones you are facing, so I can help you find ways to address them." The call to action was to use me, especially if your needs involved thinking or analysis. Even at a very young age, I can remember offering to help my friends with their homework. I was most comfortable with intellectual problems, because I had come to believe that emotions were dangerous, as the ones I was most familiar with from my childhood were anger and fear. I had learned that the best way to avoid them was to retreat into the realm of the mind.

On reflection, this narrative led me to transactional interactions, rather than deeper, more sustained relationships. Since my family never stayed anywhere very long, shorter-term transactional interactions were much safer and more effective for me than more meaningful relationships that would inevitably be disrupted.

This orientation had been recognized early on by, of all things, an aptitude test my third-grade class took to find out what professions we were most suited for. When I got my results, I was surprised and puzzled. The careers I was most suited for, it said, would be the priesthood or social work. Given that I had no religious inclination or particular desire to work with the poor, I believed it had missed the mark. Many years later, I realized that it had correctly identified my drive to help others with significant challenges—a drive that priests and social workers certainly have as well.

As it turned out, a new profession emerging at the time had not yet registered on the test developers' radar screen: management consultant. The role of a management consultant is to respond to the needs of executives facing significant challenges and help them with data and analysis. (Of course, there's more to management consulting, but this is the dimension most relevant to my personal narrative.) Therefore, it makes perfect sense that I would have gravitated to that career, starting at the Boston Consulting Group and then spending sixteen years at McKinsey & Company and thirteen years at Deloitte.

Although this personal narrative was far from optimal in terms of achieving my full potential, it did help to focus me on where and how I could have impact. While my narrative focused on threats facing others, it framed an opportunity for me, because helping executives helped me escape the dangerous quicksand of potentially hurtful emotions. It helped me survive and find meaning in a stressful world. It told me I could make a difference—but only by helping others, not by acknowledging or addressing my own needs.

This early personal narrative drove me to learn as much as I could outside of school, since I found school very limiting, while accumulating as many academic credentials as I could (three graduate degrees). It also drove me to write. I started early, at my high school newspaper. I wrote my first two books when I was still in graduate school and have written five more since (not including this one) while contributing articles and other content to a growing array of outlets, including a personal blog. I discovered that writing was a better way to fulfill my personal narrative than waiting for others to seek me out on a one-on-one basis, as it enabled me to be helpful to far more people while keeping me at an emotional distance from them.

Then, as an undergraduate, I became involved in movements. The war in Vietnam was at its height, and I helped organize resistance on my college campus. I was also drawn into the libertarian movement. (My early experience with my mother had left me with lifelong issues with authority figures of every kind.) These experiences challenged my belief that I could help people just by focusing on the mind. I found myself getting more and more drawn into the emotional lives of my movement comrades, as well as those of the people we were trying to mobilize.

A few years later, when I was working at the Boston Consulting Group, I recognized an unmet need in the business world. People were beginning to see how computers could help them in their businesses, but they were unable to get the help they needed from computer companies. This was in the late 1970s, when large mainframes were still dominant. When businesspeople spoke to sales reps, they were drowned in technobabble. What they needed was someone who could clearly communicate the benefits of computer technology to non-engineers. In 1980, I left the comfort and security of my job, moved to Silicon Valley, and with a team of three others launched a startup that helped physicians in small private practices use microcomputers to handle back-office functions like billing and insurance claim processing.

Make no mistake about it, the urge to do this was driven by my personal narrative to help others with my mind, but I couldn't do it on my own. By the time I sold the company, it had become the largest value-added reseller in its market segment, with 100 employees, all of whom were integral to its success. This experience highlighted a key limitation in my personal narrative. My call to action had been directed to those who needed my help; it didn't include people who could amplify my ability to help. As such, it inherently limited my ability to fulfill my narrative.

REFLECTING ON YOUR PERSONAL NARRATIVE

The value of this kind of self-reflection comes through in the journey of one of my clients. A doctor in her mid-30s, she practiced at one of the leading hospitals in the United States. As she had never really thought about her view of the future and her call to action, we spent some time exploring them. The answers she came up with were revealing. At first, she articulated an opportunity-based narrative: she had wanted to be in a financially rewarding profession that also helped others. But when we dug a bit deeper, she realized that her parents, who came from modest backgrounds, had been more focused on threat than opportunity. This led her to understand that she was not so much pursuing an opportunity as seeking to avoid a threat. The fear of a low-income future had driven her to seek refuge in a well-paying profession, even though the profession was not something she was passionate about.

She gained even more insight when we turned to the question of what call to action her personal narrative issued to others. She didn't have a call to action. Influenced by her parents' fear, she had come to believe that depending on others is too risky. As a result, her narrative did not call on others to support her efforts to become a successful physician; it was all on her shoulders. Worse still, she saw the people who could have helped her as potential threats, who might go after her job.

By all external indicators, my client was successful; she should have been happy. But like so many of us, she had let her fear consume her and dictate her choices. Instead of helping her rise to the challenges awaiting her, her narrative fed into her sense of fear and her pressure to perform, exacerbating both of them. As she reflected on her narrative, she began to realize that she was missing an opportunity to do more exciting and meaningful work with much greater impact.

This realization prompted her to think about what gave her the most fulfillment. She definitely felt good about helping people who were sick, but what gave her the most satisfaction was helping people stay well. This led her to frame a very different opportunity: helping patients avoid disease and improve their wellness over time. Ultimately, this motivated her to establish an independent practice whose focus was coaching people on wellness. A broad array of professionals support wellness, including meditation teachers, fitness coaches, and nutritionists. This led her to expand her personal narrative to include a call to action to others who were motivated by the same opportunity and could support her in her quest. She soon evolved a growing network of experts, which allowed her to achieve much more impact. She has now begun to recruit other physicians and coaches into her practice.

It's important to make your personal narrative explicit, because when you reflect on it, you come to understand how it might have been holding you back. You may have to evolve it before you can move past your fear and achieve your full potential, whether in your career, your life, or in the world at large.

First, ask yourself some questions to draw out your narrative. Is your view of the future driven more by an expectation of threat or opportunity? In other words, are you more concerned that the future could undermine what you have already achieved, or are you focused on an opportunity to achieve much more? Of course, we all foresee a mixture of threats and opportunities, but the key question here is which predominates: Do you feel more threatened or more excited about what's ahead?

Next, reflect on your call to action to others in this future. What role, if any, are you asking them to play? What kind of collaboration are you seeking? Perhaps most importantly, is there a compelling reason for them to act in ways that can help you and themselves address the threat or opportunity ahead?

Resist the temptation to be too conceptual or to frame what you think others would want to hear you say. Be true to yourself. Don't let your fear limit or dictate your ability to achieve more of your potential. To do that is to let fear win, which defeats the whole point of crafting a narrative. Often, we frame the opportunity too narrowly to match our true potential. Everyone's potential is ultimately unlimited; we owe it to ourselves to challenge ourselves to achieve more.

We take the first step on our new journey when we recognize the extent to which fear has shaped our narrative and the ways our narrative is reinforcing our fear. We need to shift our attention to the big opportunities we could be addressing and how much we are sacrificing by giving in to our fear. Creating a narrative is about thinking and dreaming big and preventing that nagging voice in your head from limiting your ability to accomplish your goals. Reflect on choices and actions you are facing in the days, weeks, and months ahead. Which are you likely to make, and what does that tell you about what is driving you?

Next, ask yourself what support, if any, you are seeking from others as you pursue those choices and actions. Many of us aspire to be completely self-sufficient. This limits what we want to accomplish, because we are each just one person. Don't let your fear hold you back; think about how much more you might be able to accomplish if you could motivate and mobilize others to participate in your quest. The fact is, no matter how smart and strong you are, you can achieve more of your potential if you work with others to create more effective approaches to the opportunities you want to address. You're also more likely to stay on course if you have others who support you and hold you accountable to your goals. So, are you asking for the right kind of help from the right kinds of people?

If you do have a call to action for others, reflect on whether your narrative motivates them to commit the time and effort required. Do you really understand what motivates others? Are you framing the threat or opportunity in the most inspiring way?

When I reflected on my own narrative, I saw that the pattern of placing my own needs below others' continued in my relationships with women. Toward the end of my second marriage, I experienced deep hurt and sadness, but it led me to find the strength and inner resources to be true to my needs. Asking for a divorce forced me to reflect on my narrative, to ask myself what my needs truly were. After a difficult period of self-examination, I realized I had already begun to evolve an alternative narrative, without being aware of it.

As I looked at my experiences in college and later in life, I saw that my actions had not just been about serving the needs of others. I was also addressing my need to explore new arenas and to create platforms that would help all of us—myself included—to achieve more of our potential. In the antiwar movement, I had joined a group of people who were venturing out beyond mainstream politics and creating a platform to drive significant change. Then there was my experience building a startup. I had worked not just with my founding team and our employees, but also with the network of experts we relied on and with our clients to develop a new market. When I joined McKinsey & Company, I was similarly drawn to new arenas within the firm. I helped launch two new practice areas within McKinsey and was a member of the team that founded its first office in Silicon Valley.

As I reflected on what had motivated me to participate in these initiatives, I realized I had been seeking to achieve more of my potential by venturing into uncharted territories. This led me to craft a new personal narrative that went something like this: "Let's overcome our fear and venture out onto promising edges that have the potential to change people's lives for the better." The call to action was shifting from those who needed help ("Tell me your problems, so I can help you") to those who were motivated to help ("Let's change people's lives for the better"). My personal narrative's call to action now focuses much more on the people who can come together with me to craft platforms that can help others achieve more of their potential. There's still a secondary call to action for others to use the platforms as they are deployed, but the narrative's primary focus is on those who can help me to co-create those platforms.

As we'll see in Chapter 8, the opportunities I was pursuing crystallized even more as I began to discover my passion of the explorer.

LESSONS LEARNED IN SHAPING PERSONAL NARRATIVES

Working with clients to reshape their narratives has led me to four important insights. The first insight, as I already mentioned, is that threat-based narratives are inherently limiting. Of course, threats are real and pressing, but the best way to address them is by translating them into opportunities that can be expanded over time. For example, many of us are driven by the fear we will be ostracized if we don't fit in. That's a powerful fear. But what if we shifted our focus to bringing people together in ways that allow them to complement and compound each other's unique capabilities? When we address that opportunity, we not only reduce our risk of being abandoned or ostracized but also develop much more of our potential.

Second, there's power in leverage: we can have much more impact if we can mobilize a broader and more diverse group of people to address the opportunity we have identified. We not only will have more resources but also will learn a lot faster as we come up with a wider variety of approaches to address the opportunity. Calls to action should not be one-on-one; they should address a larger group.

Third, our calls to action will achieve much more if we move beyond short-term transactional relationships and build long-term, trust-based relationships instead. Sure, we can be helpful to each other in the moment, addressing opportunities and challenges as they arise. But deeper relationships cultivate a much deeper understanding of who we are, what our respective limitations and capabilities are, and what can really motivate us.

Finally, our personal narrative will have much more impact if we can frame the opportunity at its core in a way that shows how it supports and enhances a broader range of opportunities. We need to keep our personal narrative tightly focused on the opportunity that excites us the most, but we should explore its connections with others. In my case, the opportunity of venturing out onto edges with the potential to change lives for the better connected to opportunities to transform institutions in ways that would help people learn faster, create more inclusive and prosperous societies, and cultivate more sustainable ecosystems that better support the planet.

BOTTOM LINE

Whether we know it or not, we all have a personal narrative that is shaping our lives, our careers, the causes we dedicate ourselves to, and all the other opportunities we pursue, for better or for worse. There's enormous value in examining the key choices and actions in our life to make explicit the narrative that has driven them. As you reflect on your personal narrative, here are some key questions to ask:

- **Have I identified a big enough opportunity?**
- **Does the opportunity really excite me?**
- **Am I issuing a call to action to the people who can be most helpful in accomplishing it?**
- **Have I framed the opportunity in the best way to motivate others to take action with me?**

Remember, the key focus of a personal narrative is a call to action issued to others. When we address a big enough opportunity and motivate and mobilize others to join us in our quest to address it, we can achieve much more of our potential.

CHAPTER 3

INSTITUTIONAL NARRATIVES

The Power of Leverage

Narratives are not just for individuals. Institutions also can increase their impact and address significant emerging opportunities by creating effective narratives. This is true for entrepreneurial and incumbent businesses, nonprofits, government agencies, and schools. The whole issue of institutional narrative is a big, unaddressed space, and the institutions that find ways to craft meaningful narratives will enjoy powerful advantages over those that don't.

As we will see in Chapter 6, personal narratives and institutional narratives are even more impactful when they are aligned. The personal narratives of institutional leaders can become the seedbeds for inspiring institutional narratives, which can help other individuals catalyze their own narratives in turn. But first, this chapter helps you recognize, understand, and craft institutional narratives.

THE "PSEUDO-NARRATIVES" OF INSTITUTIONS TODAY

Like individuals, institutions have implicit narratives but rarely take the time and effort to make them explicit. This may not be a bad thing, because most institutions' narratives are embarrassingly narrow minded and self-centered; they show very little understanding of who their stakeholders are and what their aspirations and challenges might be. Instead, it's all about them. For most, the call to action essentially reduces to "Buy (or use) my products or services." This may be one of the reasons why trust levels in institutions are declining globally.

When I speak to executives about the concept of narrative, they often respond, "Of course we have a narrative. We started in a garage; we overcame enormous obstacles and accomplished amazing things. And the narrative is open ended; there's a lot more to be accomplished and great opportunities in the future." Yes, it's open ended, but what is the call to action to those outside the corporation? "Watch in awe as we accomplish more amazing things"? It's all about the institution and what it hopes to accomplish.

WHAT MAKES AN INSTITUTIONAL NARRATIVE EFFECTIVE?

An effective institutional narrative focuses on opportunities that are meaningful for the organization's customers or, in the case of nonbusinesses, the people they serve. While the opportunity ultimately bears some relationship to the organization's products and services, it needs to be framed much more broadly so that it speaks to the aspirations and needs of the people being addressed. Based on a deep understanding of their needs, the narrative should identify an inspiring opportunity for them and an explicit call to action they can take to address it. That action should go well beyond buying products or services.

Not many institutional narratives illustrate the potential of narratives as I describe them, but some do. A good example is Apple's early slogan "Think Different." Unpack it, and a very powerful and inspiring narrative emerges. Apple's marketing campaign celebrated bold, undaunted, and creative "crazy ones" like Einstein, Picasso, Bob Dylan, and Muhammed Ali—great individuals who stand in stark contrast to life in the world created by the first generation of digital technology. Early computers and automation replaced our names with numbers, stuck us in cubicles, and made us cogs in machines. But Apple's institutional narrative indicated that things have changed. A new generation of digital technology has placed the most powerful tools we can imagine at our fingertips, giving us the opportunity to express our unique individuality and creativity. But that opportunity isn't guaranteed; it requires us to think and act differently. Are we prepared to take up the challenge? It's up to us to pursue it.

This narrative speaks to a deep and aspirational quality in many of us, and it came at a critical moment in time, when the counterculture era was ending and a new era of corporate conformity was beckoning. Because Apple tapped into our cherished sense of individuality, its narrative resonated deeply. Critically, the narrative was not about Apple per se. It was about all of us. Yes, the company had some products that could help us express ourselves, but that wasn't the point. The point was that we had to act.

And this narrative wasn't just a script crafted by a PR firm. If you wanted to see two people who thought and acted differently, you could not find two better examples than Steve Wozniak and Steve Jobs. Neither of the Steves told their own stories, however. Instead, the commercial flashed images of iconoclasts like Martin Luther King Jr., Maria Callas, Mohandas Gandhi, Amelia Earhart, and Frank Lloyd Wright. The point wasn't that they would have used Apple computers if those had been available. Rather, it was that they were able to achieve enormous impact by thinking differently in many different domains. Individual expression and creativity were an opportunity for everyone.

Apple's slogan provides a great example of how stories can be used to reinforce and strengthen a broader narrative. The stories of the people in Apple's "Think Different" campaign give credibility to the narrative, and the narrative makes the stories even more powerful, because they are not just isolated examples of what people accomplished. Rather, they are illustrations of what *you* can accomplish if you heed the call to action.

Another company that developed a powerful narrative is Nike, with its slogan "Just Do It." That slogan was a summary of the call to action for a rich and relevant narrative that could be summarized this way: So many things compete for our time that we've lost sight of what's really important to us. Tied to our desks, we neglect our bodies. We are not just sacrificing our health and wellness, but also depriving ourselves of the exhilaration that accompanies physical exercise.

The opportunity framed by Nike's narrative is the chance to reconnect with our physical selves. We can push ourselves to new levels of physical performance, experiencing the euphoria that comes from achieving something we had never done before. We can expand our potential and lead much more fulfilling lives. But as with any opportunity, it is up to us to achieve it. The choices we make and the actions we take will determine whether we will participate in this opportunity. Instead of procrastinating or overthinking it, we should *just do it*. Carve out the time, set a high bar for ourselves, and act.

Nike used stories to give life to this narrative, enlisting a broad range of athletes, including soccer greats Ronaldinho and Wayne Rooney, basketball stars Michael Jordan and Kobe Bryant, and tennis stars Roger Federer and Rafael Nadal, to illustrate what can be accomplished when you just do it. But the stories were not targeting professional athletes. They were targeted to all of us, with the message that all of us can do more than we think.

Another example of an institutional narrative comes from Airbnb. Four years ago, Airbnb crafted a narrative that was captured in the slogan "Belong anywhere." Once again, it can be unpacked into a narrative that goes like this: A long time ago, we all lived in small communities, where we had deep connections with our neighbors. Now most of us live in large cities, where paradoxically, we are more isolated. We travel to see new places and expand our horizons, but we are always "outsiders"—tourists who do not truly belong. Our experiences would be so much richer if we were able to connect with the communities we visit, building relationships that last well beyond our visit. We can, in fact, belong anywhere, but it won't happen automatically. We need to take the actions required to make those connections.

In each of these three examples, the slogan powerfully distills the call to action. Its full meaning is unlocked in the context of the opportunities framed by the narrative—why those opportunities are so important, the roadblocks and obstacles that can stand in the way of attaining them, and the actions that people must take to seize the opportunities. There's a dramatic arc to the institutional narrative that gives the call to action its power.

THE DISTINCTION BETWEEN NARRATIVE AND PURPOSE

A narrative is different from a purpose. These days, purpose is a hot topic. We have a hunger to commit ourselves to something meaningful that can have significant and lasting impact. More and more institutions are focused on defining and communicating their purpose.

The way most institutions define it, purpose is about the impact they want to achieve. An institution's messaging about its purpose is generally directed to the people within the organization, although messages to stakeholders outside the organization (for example, investors, partners, customers) can help them better understand its goals. Usually, however, the call to action is directed toward employees and prospective employees.

Narratives are bigger and broader than purpose statements. They are a call to action to achieve something that extends well beyond the institution, and they are intended for people who do not work in it. That said, they do create a powerful framework in which to present a purpose, because a narrative can turn the purpose into a part of something much bigger. Apple's narrative, which is to help people think differently, reclaiming their individuality and unleashing more of their potential amplifies its internal purpose—to design and deliver digital technology that can be accessed by all of us as individuals.

Purpose is certainly helpful in motivating employees. It focuses efforts within the organization, inspires the employees, and clarifies the role the organization can play in a much broader narrative. A purpose can be consistent with and contribute to a broader narrative. But it's not the narrative. It is, or should be, the derivative of a narrative.

To be confident that its purpose can really make a difference in the world, a company first needs to understand the aspirations and needs of its target customers. What opportunities are these people likely to confront? What actions do they need to be taking to address these opportunities? Once we have clarity about who we are trying to serve and what they hope to accomplish in their lives, we can begin to think about a purpose that really matters. We need to work from the outside in to ensure that we are maximizing our potential for impact.

WHY DO INSTITUTIONAL NARRATIVES MATTER?

Institutional narratives matter because they mobilize people around an opportunity that benefits themselves and the company. These narratives harness the power of pull by drawing a growing number of individuals to the company, where they can achieve more of their potential and help the company to do the same. Institutional narratives can become a powerful source of learning and loyalty. Let's take a closer look at what they have the power to do.

Tap into Exponential Leverage to Do More with Less

By defining a meaningful and inspiring opportunity to people outside the company, narratives motivate them to invest their time and resources to address it. Take the example of "Think Different," which motivated people around the world to find ways to think in creative ways. Some of them became application developers who helped expand the utility of Apple's core technology products. In some ways, these third parties invested even more of their time and resources into expanding Apple's capabilities than Apple did itself, giving it incredible leverage.

As Apple's example demonstrates, narratives can help organizations accelerate their progress and impact, because they mobilize a much larger ecosystem that harnesses network effects in which the value created and the impact achieved increase exponentially as the number of participants rises. This makes it harder for "fast followers" to catch up and can deliver a competitive in today's fast-paced, high-pressure business environment, in which it is no longer enough to simply follow a linear path, improving by increments.

Accelerate Learning

If narratives are properly framed, they can unleash a wave of experimentation, tinkering, and exploration that can lead to breakthrough insights from unexpected quarters. Tapping into this exponential leverage, companies can pursue powerful shaping strategies that restructure whole industries. That is what Apple did. As more and more users discovered and modeled new ways of thinking and acting, a rich and diverse collection of developers created a growing array of innovative applications. Some of those innovators achieved greater impact than others, but everyone learned faster by observing and reflecting on what worked and what didn't.

The point is that even the smartest of us no longer have all the answers. We need to tap into a much broader community of expertise and capability to help us come up with the next wave of insights, practices, and products.

Build Loyalty and Trust, Leading to Long-Term Relationships

Calls to action are in effect calls for help. They declare that the opportunity addressed by the narrative cannot be achieved by the organization alone. That expresses vulnerability, which builds trust, and the value of trust cannot be overestimated. Apple users became intensely loyal, paying premium prices not just for personal computers but also for the company's iPods, iPads, and iPhones.

In our Big Shift world, trust in all our institutions is eroding. Along with fear, other factors reducing trust include the growing realization that our institutions are too inward looking, driven by a scalable efficiency model that focuses on operating cost. The irony is that, in a rapidly changing world, this model is becoming less and less efficient. With so much competition for customers' attention, institutions need deep, long-term, trust-based relationships to be successful. These relationships can be very challenging to build and even more difficult to maintain.

Narratives provide a framework of shared commitment to an opportunity, ensuring that relationships are more enduring than the commercial ones that fray as soon as the tide changes. By working together to achieve an exciting opportunity, we get to know each other in far deeper ways than we ever would through casual conversations, which helps build trust. And by building trust, narratives help overcome fear, since now we no longer feel alone.

Strengthen Differentiation and Attract More People

With so many options competing for attention, a powerful narrative can differentiate a company from its competitors, helping it stand out from the crowd. A narrative, which is by definition a long-term, sustainable call to action, far outlives any individual product or service offering—although, of course, the evolving product or service offering must be consistent with the narrative. More importantly, the differentiation is based on a deep understanding of what drives the customer, whether it's help in solving a problem or a way to meet a need.

As difficult as it is to push your message out to an increasingly saturated audience, narratives are shared by word of mouth. Customers will swarm to you, drawn by the opportunity and the challenge you offer. When a narrative taps into a deep need, people will find you wherever you are.

Overcome Cognitive Biases

So far, I've framed the power of narrative in terms of the benefits of connecting with and mobilizing others beyond the boundaries of the institution. But there's another benefit that encompasses people within the institutions and those outside the institution. Narratives help us overcome the cognitive biases that tend to take hold in times of growing uncertainty. While completely understandable and natural, biases such as risk aversion, a shortened time horizon, and a zero-sum view of the world can cause dysfunctional behavior. If executives want to build institutions that not only can stay afloat but also grow stronger in turbulent times, they must find ways to help both their employees and the people they are trying to serve overcome the turbulence. Having a powerful narrative can help.

Shift Emotions

Most fundamentally, opportunity-based narratives can help people shift their dominant emotion from fear to hope and excitement. Those who make this shift will likely feel deep gratitude to the institution that helped them do it. For example, many parents are concerned that their schools are not adequately preparing their children for the challenging world evolving around them. A company might craft a narrative focusing on the opportunity for children to learn all the time, not just when they are in school, and the role parents and other family members can play in fostering a motivation to learn. If the company provides some products and services that help children and their family members foster that learning outside of school, the families are likely to be grateful for becoming aware of the opportunity and getting help along the way. Many will become avid ambassadors for the company and share stories about the opportunities they were able to address.

CHALLENGES IN CRAFTING A POWERFUL INSTITUTIONAL NARRATIVE

Crafting a powerful institutional narrative is easier said than done. Many companies fail to create effective narratives because they've lost touch with the people they are trying to reach. Beyond that, the leadership team must be willing to venture out of their comfort zones on multiple levels, but many are too risk-averse to do so. I've also seen the following issues get in the way of an effective narrative:

- **Over-delegating.** Often, when institutional leaders learn about the concept of narratives, they call up their PR agency and ask them to write a narrative. While PR and marketing folks can be helpful in crafting the prose, the content must come from the leadership group itself. A successful narrative requires the deep understanding, commitment, and engagement of the entire leadership team. The whole group must be aligned around a single narrative if it is to be credible to those outside the institution.

- **Not taking an outside-in perspective.** Institutional leaders are understandably focused on their institution and what's required for its success. As a result, they are prone to an inside-out perspective, meaning they are focused on what their institution can do and what is required for its success. But the power of a narrative hinges on its understanding of the aspirations and frustrations of those it is addressing outside the organization. To craft a successful narrative, leaders must start from the outside, focusing on the key stakeholders and the biggest opportunities these stakeholders might address. Then they need to look within to determine whether they have the capabilities to achieve the opportunities and goals that are most meaningful to their stakeholders. The resulting narrative might catalyze the institution to develop a new set of capabilities that can help it grow.

- **Failing to look broadly outside the institution.** When leaders look outside their institutions, they tend to focus exclusively on those they intend to serve. This causes them to overlook opportunities to mobilize third-party contributors, who may in fact be assets to the opportunity outlined in their narrative. This is a gross oversight and can cause companies to lose their biggest stakeholders. For example, a bank focusing on the opportunity for its clients to get more value and comfort from the homes they own will be tempted to focus narrowly on the financial returns from home ownership and overlook the opportunity to inspire and mobilize a broad range of third parties who can help homeowners get more enjoyment from their homes. Recall that one of the most effective elements of Apple's narrative was that it inspired a growing range of third-party developers to think differently and come up with creative new applications.

- **Failing to connect the opportunities.** Because narratives become more effective when the opportunities that define them can be connected with an even broader range of opportunities, institutions need to look outside in crafting their narrative. What other opportunities are meaningful to people? How can the potential connections across some of these opportunities be made more explicit?

- **Not looking out to the future.** As institutional leaders craft their narrative, they must resist short-term thinking. The most powerful narratives look out to the future, identifying emerging opportunities that will become larger and larger over time. Since narratives play out over an extended period, the leaders of the organization must understand how their external stakeholders' aspirations and frustrations will evolve over time, rather than focusing narrowly on what they are today.

- **Not walking the walk.** Perhaps the most important element of crafting a narrative is institutional leaders living their narratives, as Apple's two Steves did. If their external stakeholders don't see them acting to address the opportunities in their narrative, the narrative will be quickly dismissed as just another marketing ploy. In contrast, if they see the leaders striving to achieve the opportunity in their own lives, it will further inspire them to take actions of their own.

CRAFTING AN INSTITUTIONAL NARRATIVE

As with the personal narrative, crafting an institutional narrative is an internal process that requires a lot of introspection.

In this case, it involves thinking about your company, its goals, and the goals of your employees and stakeholders. Ask yourself a series of questions:

- Who will be our most important customers and stakeholders in the next decade?

- What opportunities could we help these customers and stakeholders address that will allow them to achieve the most impact?

- What actions will they need to take in order to address these opportunities?

- What obstacles and challenges will they face? How can we inspire them to overcome those difficulties?

To help you get started on crafting your own company's narrative, the remainder of this chapter offers a few examples of institutional narratives.

Sample Narrative for a Healthcare Provider

A healthcare provider might craft a narrative like the following one to address a significant opportunity for its clients:

> Throughout history, we've focused on treating disease. We take a reactive approach, waiting until we get sick before we act. But medical science is on the cusp of a big shift. Technology is now being developed that will allow us to monitor our physical condition in real time, giving us much greater insights into what promotes our health and well-being, as well as early warnings when something

goes wrong, through an expanding array of mobile digital devices. We can now take timely action to further improve our physical condition. This allows you to take proactive measures to ensure your wellness. Those actions might be on our own or in collaboration with a growing array of wellness providers. The exciting opportunity is to tailor our wellness approaches to our unique individual circumstances and to evolve those approaches as our circumstances change. Of course, we're all going to get sick at some point in our lives, but we'll recover faster with fewer complications if we've invested the time and effort to get to know our bodies when they're healthy and to understand more deeply what they require to become even healthier. We need to view ourselves as unique individuals with distinctive requirements to achieve and maintain our health.

None of this is a given. It requires commitment and effort from all of us, but by working together and reaching out to others who can help, we can begin to discern the drivers of wellness and more rapid recoveries from illnesses.

This narrative might be best captured by the slogan "Focus on wellness, rather than illness." It speaks to a very meaningful opportunity for the organization's clients: avoidance of getting sick in the first place. The healthcare provider could benefit enormously by deploying the array of new services that monitor clients' physical condition in real time and by coaching clients in how to improve their wellness, based on their unique circumstances. The healthcare provider could also create a large network of more specialized wellness providers and collect commissions on the services they supply. Between the narrative and its expanded services, the healthcare company would build deeper relationships with its clients, motivating them to recommend the company to others.

Sample Narrative for a Bank.

Here is a narrative that a bank might craft to address a significant opportunity for its clients:

> For more than a century, our lives have followed a similar script. We went to school to prepare for a job that would last a lifetime. It might not be the most satisfying work, but it would provide us with a reliable paycheck. Then we would reap a nice pension that would allow us to play golf or bridge during our (regrettably short) golden years.
>
> That's all changing now. Thanks to science and medicine that keep us healthier longer, we now have an opportunity to craft another chapter of our lives, one that might last almost as long as our first career. If we want, we can reorder our lives around a passion that makes a larger and larger difference in the world around us. To take advantage of this new opportunity, we'll need to plan to make sure that our financial resources are sufficient.
>
> But why wait for retirement? Why settle for collecting a paycheck and being stressed by the uninteresting work we do? Digital technology is reducing barriers to entry in market after market. We first saw the effects in media businesses like filmmaking and writing, but now it is transforming industries as diverse as manufacturing and medicine, allowing anyone with a passion to gain access to the means of production and start a business of their own.

Given these new developments, why don't you step back now and think about what you're passionate about? In the next few years, you could craft a path that allows you to integrate that passion with a new profession. Why not start connecting with people who share your passion today?

This is an exciting opportunity, but it's not going to happen automatically or easily. To take advantage of it, you'll need to carefully assess the resources you have and find ways to augment them so that you'll have a cushion as you make the shift.

Such a narrative might be captured by the slogan "Pursue your passion."

This narrative by a bank is paradoxical, because it argues that money and security aren't everything. But done well, it could deepen and expand its relationships with its clients. The clients would be less inclined to see the bank from a transactional view (getting higher interest on deposits and lower interest on loans), regarding it instead as a partner that can help them pursue a more fulfilling life. At the same time, the bank would gain a market for the advisory and other financial services customers would need as they make the shift inspired by the narrative. The bank would also benefit from the referrals it would receive when it proves that it really understands what it is important to its clients.

Sample Narrative for a Battery Vendor

It's comparatively easy for healthcare providers and banks to find important and exciting opportunities. What about companies whose work is less intrinsically inspiring? Let's take the example of a company that sells a mundane item—batteries. What might that company's narrative look like?

It could begin by observing that throughout history, humans have been prisoners of their technology:

> From the time humans began to grow crops through the industrial era, we were tied to the means of production. It got worse over time. As electricity made its way into our lives, we became prisoners of our homes: if we wanted to watch a movie or listen to music, we could go only as far as the electrical cord plugged into the wall socket would allow.
>
> But that's changing now, thanks to advances in battery technology. We now have a growing opportunity to go anywhere anytime, to free ourselves of physical constraints while staying connected to all the electronic resources we need. What does this make possible? We can enjoy a greater diversity of experiences, learn faster, and have an even greater impact on those around us. That's the real opportunity—to have a greater impact, one that would have been impossible when we had to choose between staying tethered to an electrical outlet and having freedom of movement.
>
> Now we can take everything with us. Instead of waiting for people to come to us, we can go to them, bringing all the resources, experiences, information, and applications required to do whatever needs to be done.

Once again, we can capture this rich narrative in a slogan: "Expand your horizons to have more impact."

Sample Narrative for Business-to-Business Companies

The examples I've given are all in the consumer space, because that's easiest for most people to relate to, but equally powerful narrative opportunities are possible in the business-to-business (B2B) space. B2Bs' narratives also speak to people outside the company crafting the narrative, but in the context of their jobs with other companies. Typically, the people addressed in these narratives are the decision makers responsible for purchasing the product or service the company offering the narrative supplies and the people who use the product or service in their work.

As in the consumer space, the challenge is to pull back from the narrow product or service. We need to understand the context of the people we're trying to reach, so we can identify the broader opportunities that might be available to them in their work environment—opportunities that would motivate them to achieve even greater impact and, in the process, take their companies to a new level. The goal is to excite them about the possibilities and help them to think and act in a more powerful way.

Here's a sample B2B narrative for a company that designs and sells sensor technology that monitors work environments:

We live in a world of mounting pressure that requires us to accelerate our learning and constantly improve our performance. The good news is that a growing range of technology can capture data, analyze data, and deliver real-time insights into your work environment, process it, and give you rich and actionable feedback. We need to pay more attention to what is going on around us, act more quickly to gather information, and then reflect on the results, so we can refine our approaches to generate even more impact.

The call-to-action slogan of this narrative might be something like "Accelerate your performance by gaining more insight into your work environment."

The sensor technology company that is framing the narrative would benefit from focusing its business customers on the value created by learning and performance improvement. When customers understand that, they will be willing to pay a premium for the product.

Even the most humdrum products and services can be supported by a powerful narrative. The challenge is to avoid making the opportunity so generic that it loses its ability to inspire. Companies need to make the call to action so tangible that it inspires people to act.

BOTTOM LINE

Few institutions today have effective narratives. If you are affiliated with an institution, here are some key questions you should consider as you develop your institutional narrative:

- **Do we have an explicit narrative with an explicit call to action that goes beyond "buy our products" for a large number of people outside our organization?**

- **Is our narrative as powerful as it could be? Could we be addressing even bigger and more inspiring opportunities that are more meaningful to the people we are trying to reach?**

- **Are we actively capturing and communicating stories of people who have already achieved impact by taking action to address the opportunity framed by the narrative?**

- **Have we framed a statement of purpose that is clearly linked to our institutional narrative? Have we made the effort to show how that purpose is connected to our broader narrative?**

- **Are people within our company taking action in ways that are consistent with the narrative and purpose and demonstrating our commitment to that narrative?**

CHAPTER 4

GEOGRAPHICAL NARRATIVES

Drawing People Together

Cities, regions, and countries have always used narratives to harness the power of pull—drawing their own people closer together, attracting value-adding people from other parts of the world, and inspiring others who cannot make the journey but can help it in other ways. People visit Las Vegas for the freewheeling fun that they might prefer will "stay in Vegas," and people have supported the nation of Israel for its religious and cultural heritage.

These geographical narratives are powerful, because emotions are highly contagious. If we live in a geography where the narrative is threat based and the dominant emotion is fear, we are much more likely to feel the fear, and overcoming it will be more difficult. An example is referring to parts of the United States as the "Rust Belt." For residents of these areas, using the narrative implicit in that label can intensify fears that they will soon lose their jobs and their children will struggle. Similarly, countries that focus on the hostility

THE JOURNEY BEYOND FEAR

of neighboring countries evolve narratives that emphasize threat and cultivate the fear of loss of life.

Geographical narratives can play a significant role in helping us overcome fear, especially if the geography we live in has evolved an opportunity-based narrative. In that case, we are much more likely to be surrounded by people who are pursuing opportunities. The actions of such people and the impact they achieve can encourage our own journey beyond fear, even if we pursue different opportunities. Beyond that, an opportunity-based geographical narrative can become a catalyst for creating our own personal or institutional narrative. We could find the opportunity it holds out so inspiring that it motivates us to take bold action and overcome our fear.

REGIONAL NARRATIVES

Consider the narrative of Silicon Valley, the part of the world that has helped to shape my life. For decades, observers and analysts have puzzled over what caused this part of the San Francisco Bay Area to become such a hub of innovation and how it has sustained its innovative energy over such a long period of time. Many elements help explain its success, including the presence of Stanford and UC Berkeley, world-class universities, and its famously open culture, which encourages engineers to reach out and collaborate on overcoming whatever problems they encounter. But one element has so far escaped much notice: the narrative that shaped Silicon Valley's evolution.

If Silicon Valley had a slogan, it might be "Change the world." Unpack it, and the narrative would go something like this:

> Our world faces huge challenges and opportunities, and we urgently need technology and tools that can address them effectively. Previous generations of impressive technologies, such as the steam engine and electricity, have improved conditions globally, but always within limits. The initial burst of innovation that gave birth to each of them led to extraordinary improvements in price and performance, which quickly leveled off.
>
> Now an expanding array of digital technologies are generating exponential rates of improvement that show no signs of leveling off. These give us the ability to address challenges and opportunities that would have been viewed as insurmountable in the past. We can change the world for the better, but it's not going to happen automatically. You have to come to Silicon Valley and join in the effort to innovate. Are you willing to come here? Will you come here?

The power of this narrative draws people to Silicon Valley from all over the world. In fact, the majority of successful Silicon Valley entrepreneurs were not born in the United States, much less Silicon Valley. They came here from many different countries, drawn by the opportunity to play a role in changing the world for the better. A key contributor to Silicon Valley's success is the geographic diversity of its entrepreneurs. They brought very different experiences, perspectives, and ideas with them as they made the journey to the region.

There has also been an interesting development over time. After these immigrants achieve success, many decide to return to their home countries to launch even more startups. They remain connected to the entrepreneurial infrastructure of Silicon Valley, including venture capitalists and specialized marketing agencies who can help them scale their new startups, and they evangelize the Silicon Valley ethos. As a result, an increasingly rich global network of entrepreneurs now extends from Israel to Berlin and London and reaches deep into India, China, South Korea, and Japan. Meanwhile, budding entrepreneurs still make the journey to Silicon Valley, drawn by the narrative that inspires them to change the world.

The Silicon Valley narrative derives some of its endurance and power from the stories it integrates. When first-generation startups like AMD, Intel, and Fairchild Semiconductor became profitable by designing and making innovative semiconductors (microchips), stories about them spread. Inspired by those stories, new waves of entrepreneurs focused on hardware, application software, and platforms to leverage the growing power of semiconductors. As they succeeded in turn, the Silicon Valley narrative became ever more credible and inspiring.

How did the Silicon Valley narrative emerge? Through beliefs and action. No one sat down and wrote it out. What people wrote about was the amazing improvement in performance of digital technology. Perhaps the most famous framing of this performance improvement is Moore's law, formulated in 1965 by Gordon Moore, the cofounder of Intel, who observed that the number of transistors per square inch on an integrated circuit was doubling roughly every two years.

This wasn't a call to action. Moore was simply describing the opportunity for exponential performance improvement.

Early on, there were indications that a broader narrative was emerging. For example, Moore also said that "the revolutionaries in the world today" were engineers, rather than "the kids with the long hair and beards." At the time—the mid-1960s—there was an interesting convergence of the counterculture and engineers. Many of the early entrepreneurs in Silicon Valley were driven by very different cultural values than their parents. "Power to the people," a slogan of the counterculture, resonated with many of the early engineers in Silicon Valley. Groups like the Homebrew Computer Club were driven by a desire to take digital technology out of the back offices of large corporations and make it accessible to everyone.

These early engineers and entrepreneurs were convinced that digital technology had power far beyond what anyone could imagine at the time. Soon enough, word of their early successes spread, and the call to action began to take shape. Then the cascade of new entrants grew. Thanks to the openness of the culture, they were able to learn from and build on each other's successes.

The opportunity to change the world for the better was open ended; there was no limit to its potential. In fact, the more people who joined the quest, the bigger and more feasible its goals became. The emerging geographical narrative unleashed powerful network effects. Once it achieved critical mass, the growth in the value created became exponential, rather than simply increasing linearly with the number of people. This made it much harder for other regions to compete.

Silicon Valley's opportunity-based narrative has been key to its growth and success, but at least as important is the role it plays in shaping personal and institutional narratives. Inspired by the broader opportunity of the regional narrative, entrepreneurs crafted for themselves and their companies' narratives that focused on a component of that broader opportunity. As I discussed earlier, Apple crafted a narrative that focused on the opportunity to achieve more by thinking differently. Google's founders focused on the opportunity to learn faster by leveraging the power of the internet to access a broader and broader array of information.

CITY NARRATIVES

Perhaps even more interesting than narratives of regions, such as Silicon Valley, are the city narratives that have emerged and evolved throughout history. For example, we can note the role that specific cities have played in the evolution of Western civilization. We could start with Athens in the classical era, then move on to Florence at the beginning of the Renaissance, Paris at the onset of the Enlightenment, and Vienna as one of the key seedbeds for Modernism in the late 19th and early 20th centuries. The rise and influence of these cities were shaped by their powerful narratives, which drew people to them and influenced many more all over the world.

Let's look at the narrative that emerged in Florence in the 14th century. While Florence was already prosperous, its narrative encouraged its residents to expand their merchant networks across the world and address unmet needs by coming up with more creative business propositions. This stimulated considerable experimentation and evolution in the textile industry, which was the core of Florence's economy. A virtuous cycle resulted: the more wealth that was created, the more money was available to support artists and scientists, which encouraged businesspeople and artisans to become more creative themselves. Ultimately, it changed the entire world.

Many historians focus on the art and architecture that defined Florence in the 15th century, created by such talents as da Vinci, Michelangelo, Botticelli, Brunelleschi, Ghiberti, Donatello, and Masaccio. But it was the great writers of the previous century—including Dante, Petrarch, and Bocaccio—who outlined a worldview that incorporated the wisdom of the ancient Greeks and Romans with a new scientific spirit and a call to expand the vast intellectual and creative potential they believed God had given humanity. That ethos made Florence the cradle of the Renaissance. What was the narrative that emerged from these early writings? It might be summarized in the slogan "Explore everywhere to express more of your human potential."

Unpack that, and something like the following narrative begins to emerge:

> We are emerging from an era that confined us to a narrow set of religious texts and kept us focused on God rather than ourselves. We humans accumulated so much wisdom and insight in the Greek classical era; we need to rediscover that to begin our journey. But there is so much more that we can learn by exploring the world within and around us, finding new ways to express our humanity. To do that, we must venture beyond the accepted and the familiar. Are you willing to take that risk? Will you take that risk?

As with all geographical narratives, it is interesting to speculate what factors led Florence to become the source of this narrative. Many elements came together. First, Florence was among the largest and most rapidly growing cities in Europe at the time. Moreover, it was one of the leading merchant republics, which characterized the development of Italy at that time. While they were certainly not democracies, they offered much more freedom of expression than the political structures that characterized most feudal societies. They were also gathering spots for traders from the rest of Europe and beyond. This exposed them to a wide variety of cultures and perspectives, making it more and more difficult to remain hidden within the cloisters of the church.

The growth of trade and finance generated increasing wealth within some of Florence's leading families, most notably the Medicis, who became patrons of artists and architects, as well as other intellectuals, providing them with the opportunity to express their creativity. There was also an important element of competition, as these families sought to fund the most impressive artistic and architectural creations. Not only the families were competing; the artists, architects, and writers also were competing with each other to evolve their expressive techniques to higher and higher levels. As more people were exposed to this kind of creative expression, they too were inspired to heed the call to action of the narrative. The invention (or reinvention) of the printing press in 1454 helped the narrative gather momentum and spread, as people throughout Europe gained access to the ideas and insights emerging in Florence without having to travel there. The spread of the narrative was also enhanced by the growth of libraries.

The rise and fall of Savonarola in the 1490s marked Florence's retreat as a leader of the Renaissance, but by then the narrative had been propagated. The Northern Renaissance took hold in the Low Countries of Europe and then spread into France, Germany, England, Poland, and the Scandinavian countries, leading to significant advances in science in such fields as chemistry, medicine, and astronomy.

NATIONAL NARRATIVES

Countries also have narratives. Take the example of the United States. Its growth depended critically on a narrative that had global appeal and drew an increasing number of people to its shores.

Once again, no one penned the narrative, it emerged over time. Its call to action was simple and compelling: "Come to America to achieve your dreams." Behind that call was a narrative:

> Human history is full of religious, political, and economic oppression that, at best, has limited people's ability to achieve their potential and, at worst, has led to grinding poverty and massacres. America offers a prospect of unprecedented freedom (well, unless you are a Native American, black, or a woman) to pursue your beliefs and dreams and achieve unimagined success and impact in the areas that matter the most to you. But you have to be willing to make the journey. Are you willing to tear yourself out of the home and community you grew up in and venture halfway across the world to make a new start in a new land? Will you?

This was an extraordinarily powerful narrative that drew people from all over the world. It flooded the United States with talent that built a prosperous economy that rapidly spread across the continent. It gave the United States a profound advantage over other countries, as it attracted their best and brightest and most motivated. Remember, settlers first came to the New World when agriculture still dominated. The European aristocracies were based on land ownership; in the New World, anyone could carve a farm out of the wilderness if they were brave and determined enough. Not only that, but also the colonists had challenged the greatest power on earth and won their independence. If they could do that, anything was possible.

Why are national narratives important? Because they amplify personal and institutional narratives. The US national narrative inspired people to overcome their fear and make a long journey to an unknown land to pursue their dreams. It inspired many of them to build businesses. This in turn gave rise to institutional narratives that focused on opportunities for others. Once again, network effects took hold: as more people made the journey, still more people were inspired to take risks in pursuit of their dreams. National narratives like that of the United States play into the idea that you can expand your narrative into something bigger and greater than yourself.

SHAPING GEOGRAPHICAL NARRATIVES

As we've seen, geographical narratives can be great drivers of prosperity, as they catalyze creativity and innovation, harnessing the power of pull by drawing talent from far and wide to compete and collaborate, amplifying each other's efforts. Once unleashed, the network effects can lead to an expanding and enduring impact.

The geographical narratives discussed so far in this book have been emergent; no one set out to craft them. But it may be possible to craft a geographical narrative with the intention of driving more prosperity in a given geography. Doing so would begin with the recognition that all social entities— cities, regions, and countries—already have narratives, even if they are seldom explicit. Start by surfacing the existing narrative and then build on it.

Remember, your geographical narrative should be a call to action to others; it's not about the geography itself. For example, rather than thinking about what a city says about itself, what is the city asking others to do? Many geographies are largely inward looking. They have no call to action to others. The larger the geography, the more likely this is to be the case. That's an important realization on its own. If there is no call to action to others, the geography is limiting its potential from the start.

In a world of mounting performance pressure, where talent is increasingly critical to success, all geographies should be aggressively seeking to find ways to attract talent from all over the world. The call to action should be to find ways to either draw talent to the geography or, at a minimum, motivate talent in other areas to find ways to interact with it. The places that act on this opportunity are likely to prosper, while those that don't will become more and more marginalized.

Talent is increasingly looking for opportunities to learn faster, driven by the realization that in an exponentially changing world, learning faster is a key source of advantage. If the call to action involves an opportunity to learn faster, it is much more likely to draw the talent that is already motivated to do this.

One way to evolve a more powerful geographical narrative is to reflect on what the biggest opportunity for the geography might be. Ideally, it should leverage some existing strengths or advantages it already possesses. New York, for example, is one of the biggest financial centers in the world. Rather than resting on its laurels, it might focus on the opportunity that digital technology creates to provide much greater financial value at a much larger scale and much lower cost than previously imaginable. On a related note, it might highlight the opportunity to create a more inclusive financial system, within its own boundaries and around the world, that draws in marginalized populations. Those opportunities could be sufficiently large and inspiring to draw more creative talent to New York to pursue them.

To make the narrative come alive, some targeted initiatives would be needed to demonstrate New York's commitment to it. For example, some of the key universities in the city might launch research to explore the technologies it requires. Some of its venture capitalists could create funds to support startups that seek to reinvent financial services in ways that expand their reach and effectiveness. A major financial institution might announce a crowdsourcing initiative to reimagine student loans in a way that would make them both more accessible and less of a financial burden for students after they graduate from college.

Any of these initiatives could emerge spontaneously, but they are much more likely to take hold if a small group of people comes together to imagine what these initiatives might look like and then engages the leaders who can launch them. The initiatives would be more likely to amplify and reinforce each other if they were framed as part of a broad effort, and they would have much greater impact if their early successes were publicized.

While many cities have economic-development initiatives that attempt to create and leverage a "brand," I have not been able to find any examples of full-blown geographical narratives that were consciously crafted and deployed. Still, I suspect that it might be possible for people who understand the power of narratives to come together and become a catalyst for a set of initiatives that, if successful, could cascade into a sustaining geographical narrative. My view of this potential is shaped by my experience with and study of movement narratives (the subject of the next chapter) that were consciously crafted by groups of people with an intent to draw in more and more people over time. It can be done, but it requires a special talent to be explored later.

Also, let's not forget the kinds of narratives that cities have catalyzed throughout history that helped to shape the history of humankind. As discussed earlier, these narratives were not just focused on attracting people to the city but sought to identify an opportunity or an unmet need that anyone anywhere could address.

Just as Athens became a center of philosophy, a city today could become a center of inquiry on the blurring boundaries between technology and humanity. As we integrate more and more digital technology into our bodies, becoming cyborgs, what advantages will we gain? Will we become enslaved by technology, or can we find ways to use it to develop even more of our potential? By convening a gathering of diverse thinkers on this subject, a city could potentially spearhead a new global era of ideas, much as happened in Athens, Florence, and Paris in the past. All it takes is a sense of the emerging opportunities and the ability to motivate people to become the catalysts for something bigger over time.

Do these narratives have to be geographically based? Couldn't groups come together anywhere, drawn together by their commitment to creating a new opportunity-based narrative? That's an interesting question. My take is that shared geography plays a significant role in building the deep, trust-based relationships that are the foundation of successful geographical narratives. With the deployment of ever more powerful global digital infrastructures, we can build richer and deeper relationships across great geographic distances, but at least until now, e-mail, social media, and Zoom have not been able to match the depth of relationships that form when we come together in a shared physical space. That's why cities are growing at such a rapid rate. Also, if we lose the geographic dimension to the narrative, it begins to look like a movement narrative, which requires a very different kind of organization.

BOTTOM LINE

No single institution can attract or mobilize all the talent needed to learn faster in a world of exponential change. The accelerating pace of urbanization reflects the understanding that we will learn a lot faster if we are in densely populated cities. That learning can be further amplified and accelerated if it is focused on specific opportunities that require the sustained engagement of many participants from diverse backgrounds and perspectives.

The most successful geographical narratives mobilize diverse people around a common desire to achieve an inspiring opportunity, recognizing and acknowledging that the more diverse they are, the greater the impact they can create. Cities, regions, and countries that figure out how to craft and disseminate compelling social narratives are likely to accelerate their learning and their ability to innovate, advancing to ever higher levels of achievement.

Wherever you're sitting in the world, here are some questions to ask:

- **What are the implicit narratives of the place you are located (at the levels of city, region, and country)?**

- **Do these narratives frame an opportunity that is compelling enough to talented people that it can motivate them to relocate to your area?**

- **Are some significant initiatives already under way in your area? These can help instill confidence that the opportunity is achievable.**

- **Are there stories that can be told about the impact already achieved? If so, are these stories being widely disseminated?**

- **What can be done to refine or evolve the narrative to make it even more compelling to a broader and more diverse pool of talent?**

CHAPTER 5

MOVEMENT NARRATIVES

Mobilizing People for Change

We are coming to a fork in the road. Depending on the choices we make, we can either continue to improve our condition, as we have over the past several centuries, or fall prey to a backlash that halts or reverses our progress. Those choices will be determined to a large extent by movement narratives.

Some of the most influential movements in the world today are driven by threat-based narratives that reinforce our fears and polarize us. Consider, for example, the Brexit movement in England and the movement to "build the wall" in the United States to deal with the "threat" of illegal immigrants. We need more of the kinds of opportunity-based narratives that can help us overcome our fear, tear down the barriers we hide behind, and come together to build a better world.

For that reason, this chapter is particularly important. Geographical narratives and movement narratives not only play a huge role in shaping the environments we live and operate in, but they also influence our personal and institutional narratives. We ignore them at our peril.

DEFINING MOVEMENTS

Let me begin by defining what I mean by *movements*, since that term is used loosely to mean many things. The types of movements I am concerned with are grassroots efforts to mobilize large numbers of people to pursue broad agendas for change. So my definition requires intention, unlike "movements" that emerge and gather force spontaneously, like some fads or trends in the fashion or art world, such as the bell-bottom pants that defined 1970s fashion or cubism that spread in the art world in the early 20th century. My definition excludes concerted efforts by ruling elites to drive their own agendas, like the Chavismo movement in Venezuela, or Chairman Mao's Great Proletarian Cultural Revolution. Finally, my definition specifies that a movement has a large number of independent participants, differentiating movements from efforts to drive change within a single institution, like digital-transformation programs within a company.

Movements have taken many different forms over time. The earliest were probably religious, as people inspired by certain religious beliefs attempted to convert others and change their beliefs and behaviors to create a better society. These were soon joined by political movements that attempted to achieve fundamental change in their societies. Sometimes these were driven by a desire to achieve independence from some remote power. Others were driven by a view of certain policies that were deemed necessary for the healthy functioning of society—for example, the antislavery movement, the prohibition movement, labor movements, the women's suffrage movement, civil rights movements, and peace movements. Some political movements were shaped by a much more fundamental agenda for change—for example, the Marxist and fascist movements.

I have participated in many movements and spent decades studying them throughout history and in different parts of the world. Based on this work, I have concluded that a successful movement depends on two elements. The first is a narrative that can focus and motivate participants. The second is a particular way of organizing—something I call "creation spaces" and will describe later in this chapter—that can help participants learn, amplifying their impact over time.

MOVEMENT NARRATIVES

Throughout history, movement narratives have moved millions to lay their lives on the line. Talk about emotional power: many made the ultimate sacrifice.

What are some examples of movement narratives? Let's recall the Christian religious narrative I mentioned in Chapter 1, which is just one of many religious movements throughout the world. At the risk of oversimplification, it can be summarized as follows:

> We are born in sin, but a savior came to earth to offer us the opportunity for redemption. Salvation, however, is not guaranteed; we must accept the savior and live by his teachings. Are you willing to do that? Will you?

Similarly, Buddhism teaches about Karma and the opportunity we have to come back in the afterlife in an even better situation if we live a good life. All religions craft opportunity-based narratives that offer the potential to achieve a fulfilling afterlife if we live in a certain way.

I also mentioned a political movement narrative in Chapter 1—the Marxist narrative—which says capitalism exploits and enslaves its wage workers. Marxism offers its adherents the opportunity to build a fair society in which everyone prospers. But it will not happen on its own. Workers must first come together and mobilize to overthrow the capitalist system. Their actions determine how the narrative will resolve.

These movement narratives combine elements of opportunity and threat, but the opportunity is what ultimately inspires people to act. Look at any successful movement for change throughout history, and you will see that it was driven by a compelling and energizing opportunity-based narrative that moved people to come together and act. We can learn a lot by analyzing those narratives and understanding how they might help us craft new ones to accomplish even greater things today.

As an example, one of the reasons the civil rights movement in the United States succeeded as it did was that it emphasized the opportunity that could be achieved if we all came together, rather than focusing solely on the injustice of racial discrimination. Martin Luther King Jr. was one of the key framers of its powerful narrative, which built on and strengthened the overall American narrative by highlighting the opportunity to include all those who had been excluded by prejudice and segregation.

In his powerful "I Have a Dream" speech in Washington, DC in 1963, King framed the opportunity for all people to overcome their differences, to come together as equals, and to achieve wonderful things together. He positioned this opportunity in the context of the historical American Dream to suggest that this opportunity was simply taking our historical journey to the next level.

There's a reason this is one of the most quoted speeches in American history. Its focus on opportunity was deeply inspiring and motivated people of all races to join forces to help end segregation policies.

Movement narratives take time to acquire the right structure and tone and texture. Stories can reinforce them by showing us in a very tangible way how individuals and groups successfully confronted challenges and reaped rewards. But the overarching narrative is ultimately what sustains and amplifies the impact of movements.

To be clear, the civil rights movement wasn't just Martin Luther King Jr.; it was and is a *movement*, with hundreds of thousands of dedicated participants and talented leaders, including W. E. B. Du Bois, A. Philip Randolph, and Bayard Rustin, who emerged over the decades to craft a collective narrative that spoke to a larger and larger portion of the population. And the fight to achieve full equality still continues. Its leaders and participants haven't always agreed with each other about tactics, but they are firmly united by the shared narrative that emerged from collective action and acts of enormous bravery by people like Claudette Colvin, Rosa Parks, James Meredith, and John Lewis.

But as important as opportunity-based narratives are, they are not sufficient to sustain a movement. Movements are not just about ideas and inspiration; they're about action. How do we mobilize a large number of independent participants and help them amplify their impact over time?

CELLULAR ORGANIZATION

Every movement I have participated in and all of the successful ones I've studied have had a distinctive way of organizing. Rather than a vertical hierarchy or pyramid, like you find in corporations or government, they take shape as a collection of small cells, each consisting of groups of three to fifteen people who meet regularly, often several times a week. I use the word *cells* to describe these groups in the context of movements, but as we'll see, I believe these small groups are needed to drive learning and impact in other contexts as well. In that broader context, I will refer to them as "impact groups."

These cells focus on finding pragmatic ways to take action that will have impact locally while making progress toward the broader opportunity identified by the movement narrative. They experiment with many kinds of initiatives so they can learn what works best. The members of these cells develop deep, trust-based relationships with each other, hold each other accountable to ensure that everyone is contributing, and provide emotional support for each other when things go wrong. They constantly challenge each other to come up with ever more creative ideas for actions that can achieve greater impact.

These small cells don't scale; once they grow to more than about fifteen people, the relationships among the participants fray and become less deep. Instead, the cells connect into networks. The movement scales by adding more and more cells and, where possible, finding ways for the cells to connect with each other so that they can learn from each other's experiences.

Malcolm Gladwell provides an interesting example of this cellular structure in an article in the *New Yorker* called "The Cellular Church," which addresses a key misconception about the evangelical movement. While the media tend to focus on the megachurches of pastors like Rick Warren, Gladwell urges readers to pay attention to where the real action is: in small groups of faithful who meet a couple of times each week. The goal of these groups, Gladwell said, is to work together to develop practices that can increase their impact in their local communities. The cells come together en masse on Sundays in churches and other forums to share and learn from their experiences.

Gladwell's article resonated with me, as it reminded me of my days in the anti–Vietnam War movement. Our real work wasn't carried out in the massive street demonstrations, which drew all the media attention, but in the local chapters of Students for a Democratic Society (SDS) and similar groups that were meeting and acting much more frequently to inform and mobilize people in a growing range of acts of resistance. In my research on other successful movements, I saw this same pattern of organization in action time and time again. This form of organization has also been applied broadly in self-help and human potential movements. One of the best-known examples is Alcoholics Anonymous, which organizes its participants into small groups that develop deep, trust-based relationships with one another, providing mutual support on their journeys of recovery.

Singularity University, where I teach, is an example of an institution that has harnessed this cellular form of organization. Its founders framed an inspiring narrative regarding the opportunity to create abundance via digital technology; its core offering is a growing array of educational programs. But its most important initiative is its effort to organize its alumni into cells that design and deploy programs to help them learn from each other as they work to realize those opportunities. It also created an incubator to support entrepreneurial business startups that pursue those goals. As a result, Singularity University has become the catalyst for a global movement of people and businesses.

THE POWER OF CREATION SPACES

The cellular structure of movements also aligns with research I have been carrying out on creation spaces. I originally came across creation spaces in arenas where you see rapid and sustained performance improvement. These run the gamut from extreme sports like big-wave surfing to online video games like *World of Warcraft*. As diverse as these domains are, all of them spawned environments that employ cellular forms of organization to help accelerate learning. The members of these small impact groups share their vulnerabilities in a quest to learn from each other, forming deep, trust-based relationships.

The real power of a creation space is that it establishes an environment that can scale in ways that help the small groups learn even faster by connecting with each other. They employ a variety of mechanisms to this end, ranging from regular gatherings of participants across impact groups to online discussion forums in which participants in one impact group can ask questions and get advice from participants in other groups. If you want to know more about creation spaces, I've written extensively about them in my book *The Power of Pull*.

These creation spaces offer powerful ways to overcome fear. By bringing people together into small cells, they help participants to connect in deep ways that help build trust and overcome a sense of isolation. Also, participants develop a growing awareness that the cell is not alone but supported by a growing number of other cells that are bringing more and more people together. Fear turns into excitement as participants gain greater awareness of the number of people who share their commitment to addressing the opportunity framed by the movement narrative.

TYING TOGETHER NARRATIVES AND CREATION SPACES

What's really interesting is the way movement narratives and creation spaces reinforce and amplify each other. Narratives provide the context and shared purpose that pull others into the movement and keep them motivated and focused as they encounter and deal with the myriad of unexpected obstacles standing in the way of meaningful change. Creation spaces provide an environment that encourages and supports local initiatives in collaboration with others, while also providing a much richer set of resources that local cells can draw on and learn from.

The more rapidly participants at the local level learn, the richer the overarching narrative becomes regarding the nature of the opportunity ahead and the journey that participants will need to make to achieve it. The actions undertaken by local cells provide powerful stories about the impact they have achieved. These add to the credibility of the broader narrative and strengthen the belief that it can be achieved. The more compelling the narrative becomes, the more it draws in others to participate and learn from each other.

IMPLICATIONS FOR MOVEMENT LEADERS

Leaders of successful movements weave together narratives and creation spaces in ways that reinforce and amplify each other. The leaders are not afraid to pose questions. In fact, they see questions as a powerful way to mobilize people to work and learn together. These questions can take many different forms—for example, "What would it take to . . .?" or "What might it look like if . . .?" What's key is that these questions focus people on the opportunity to change the game in a fundamental way by adopting new approaches and practices. More fundamentally, they communicate that it is not only OK but expected to ask questions rather than assume we already have all the answers. By inviting people to take the initiative in exploring potential answers, the questions also help break down traditional hierarchies, with their rote ways of thinking and being.

Successful movement leaders resist the temptation to frame the opportunity as inevitable. If the opportunity is inevitable, why would anyone invest the time and effort to participate? Instead, they adopt an appropriate balance between framing an opportunity and recognizing that there will be significant obstacles and barriers to overcome. That's what brings people out of their comfort zones and motivates them to come together to help make the opportunity become a reality. At some level, they have to believe that their participation is necessary to tilt the odds toward success. While the narrative prepares them for the possibility of failure and frustration, it frames an exciting challenge: What must we do to achieve the opportunity that is so worthy of our efforts?

Successful movement leaders will not be able to mobilize the participants they need unless they understand what motivates them. Too often, initiatives are framed in terms of how the world will benefit or how certain disadvantaged groups might benefit. It is essential to understand that different participants will see the opportunity in different ways (even if they all agree it is one that needs to be addressed) and through the lens of their own values, which must be appealed to directly. If the participants themselves will directly benefit from the envisioned change, then the movement narrative should call this to their attention.

Movement leaders should move beyond narrow cost-benefit analyses and speak to the broader emotional needs of the participants. What are their greatest aspirations? What are their deepest fears? Which of their deep-seated values are stirred by this opportunity? The most powerful movement leaders find ways to strengthen hope and diminish fear among participants, and they do so across groups that would naturally be polarized.

Successful movement leaders understand that they cannot dictate action. Instead, they must catalyze and facilitate action by deeply understanding the contexts and aspirations of all the potential participants and evolving new narratives that speak deeply to them.

Successful movement leadership is ultimately about balance. On the one hand, there is a need to focus participants on a shared outcome defined by the movement narrative. On the other, there is a need for many diverse local initiatives, so the movement can discover the actions with the greatest impact. It can't be a top-down effort, with detailed blueprints cascading down through a hierarchy. It is a much more horizontal form of mobilization, shaped by the desired outcome but driven by a growing number of local initiatives that evolve rapidly over time. Movement leaders need to empower people to think and act innovatively at every level of the movement, so they can learn faster together.

Critically, everything I have said here about movement leadership also applies to institutional leadership. Leaders of institutions—including businesses—who adopt these practices will have a much greater impact.

THE NEED FOR MOVEMENT NARRATIVES

In a world that is constantly being reshaped by exponential change, there are significant opportunities to craft movement narratives that can help us address some of the most significant global challenges—for example, broader inclusion of the world's population in economic prosperity, the elimination of hunger, and the provision of good health, clean water, and sanitation to everyone. The connectivity provided by digital infrastructures can help us scale movements much more rapidly and to a greater extent than would have been imaginable a few decades ago.

These kinds of global challenges are far beyond the ability of any one institution or region to address. They require the mobilization of many independent participants. In the absence of a compelling movement narrative and an organizational model that can support scalable learning, these challenges will be too big to be resolved.

It's not just about the challenges. Think of the opportunities: finding ways for humanity to learn faster and achieve more of its potential, increasing human longevity while improving quality of life, and deepening our understanding of the world around us, to name just a few. Opportunities connect with and support a broad range of other opportunities. For example, a movement driven by the opportunity to redesign our educational system may also foster a more prosperous economy and more vibrant communities.

As far as we've progressed over the past few centuries, it could just be the beginning. There's so much more we can accomplish.

OVERCOMING THREAT-BASED NARRATIVES

Before we can start to make progress, there's something we need to overcome. As I mentioned at the beginning of this chapter, we are coming to a major inflection, a fork in the road. Thanks to the mounting performance pressure we are experiencing, threat-based narratives are taking over our political and religious discourse. These threat-based narratives, which focus on the enemies at our gates, polarize us and blind us to the opportunities that we could be pursuing.

Many people embrace those threat-based narratives because they play to the fears that mounting pressure tends to generate. But we all hunger for hope and opportunity. We all want to accomplish more than we have in the past and achieve more of our potential. We need to find new ways to craft and propagate opportunity-based narratives that can bring us together and motivate us to accomplish the seemingly impossible.

It's no accident that two of the most popular US presidents in recent history were Barack Obama and Ronald Reagan—two men whose backgrounds, personalities, and politics could not have been more different. Nevertheless, as candidates, they both focused on the opportunities we could achieve if we came together. Obama touched a responsive chord with his campaign slogan "Yes, we can." Reagan was known for the inspiring image he adapted from the Puritan John Winthrop's famous sermon based on Matthew 5:1 ("Ye are the light of the world. A city that is set on a hill cannot be hid.") As Reagan put it, "America is a shining city upon a hill whose beacon light guides freedom-loving people everywhere." He amplified his vision, drawing on the American narrative, describing the shining metropolis as "teeming with people of all kinds living in harmony and peace; a city with free ports that hummed with commerce and creativity. And if there had to be city walls, the walls had doors and the doors were open to anyone with the will and the heart to get here." Those were images that could inspire hope and bring people together, and they resonated deeply with the electorate.

We desperately need a generation of movement leaders who can craft similarly compelling opportunity-based narratives. Ideally, they will not be running for office, because politicians' calls to action tend to be rather limited: "Vote for me on Election Day, and then watch and see what amazing things I can accomplish." We need a call to action that's more sustained and goes far beyond checking off the right choice on a ballot. We need a call to action that will motivate more and more people to come together and challenge each other to find ever more creative ways of addressing opportunities of the kind that require decades to achieve. We need a call to action that extends well beyond a single city or country, one that reaches out to people around the world. We need a call to action that will motivate us to achieve far more of our potential.

That's the real power and potential of movement narratives: they turn pressure into excitement.

RELEVANCE TO BUSINESS

A better understanding of movements can create significant opportunities for businesses. To illustrate how movements and movement narratives are relevant to business, let's revisit Apple's "Think Different" slogan. The narrative it summarized certainly helped to drive some of Apple's early success, but in my view, it achieved only a small fraction of the potential impact it could have. What was missing?

Imagine if Apple had framed its narrative as a movement narrative and focused on organizing and supporting a growing network of cells of people inspired by the opportunity to "think different." Rather than simply issuing a call to action, Apple could have played a more active role in organizing their efforts. Done in the right way, it would not have required a significant commitment of resources, because it would have leveraged the resources of the participants themselves. By helping them find each other, Apple could have been the catalyst for a growing creation space consisting of cells of people who were learning from each other and demonstrating ever more impact by thinking differently.

The personal connections these people developed with each other as they shared their efforts would have spilled over to Apple as the firm that helped them come together and achieve more of their potential. They would have become fervent evangelists for the company and its narrative.

Other businesses can harness movement narratives to leverage their impact in the markets or industries they are addressing. A bicycle maker can rally customers around an ecological theme; a natural-foods company can present themselves as the spearhead of a movement for wellness. Whether such narratives are just Madison Avenue hype or the genesis of a legitimate movement will depend in part on whether the company follows them up with real efforts to organize around its narrative. Those who craft movement narratives do not simply issue a call to action; they also play a role in organizing the people who are inspired by the opportunity and want to act on it.

By actively organizing and supporting the people inspired by their narrative, companies can build much deeper loyalty among their stakeholders and generate more revenue from the services they provide to an expanding array of cells. Even more importantly, they can tap into the network effects that emerge as more and more cells connect with each other. The potential for leverage is enormous.

Ultimately, movement-based narratives leverage a strength-in-numbers approach. When it's just us, we feel alone, and this feeds our greatest fears—failure, pressure to perform, inadequacy. But movement-based narratives have a unique ability to help us conquer those fears because they tap into something that is bigger than us. We begin to see that we are not alone and, moreover, that we can work together to overcome what frighten us.

BOTTOM LINE

Let's say we're interested in creating a movement, whether to serve a business or as an engine of social change. What are some of the tangible first steps we might take? The following brief suggestions are driven by one of my mantras: *Small moves smartly made can set big things in motion.*

First, aspiring movement leaders should bring together a small group of like-minded individuals and take on the task of crafting a short but compelling narrative that highlights the nature of the opportunity ahead, the forces making it more viable, and the obstacles likely to make it challenging to achieve. Be sure to avoid falling into oppositional (us-against-them) mindsets and languages. Remember, it's an opportunity-based narrative: not what you're against, but what you're for.

Second, circulate this draft narrative to a larger group of people. Solicit their suggestions for refinement and improvement.

Third, as people begin to indicate their support for your narrative and the opportunity it describes, encourage them to find others in their local communities who might share an interest in joining the adventure. Encourage them to meet and identify some actions they might quickly take to begin the journey. As they take these actions, encourage them to reflect on what's working, what's not working, and how they might refine their initiatives to achieve even greater impact.

Fourth, create some discussion forums or workspaces where these people can share their stories of success and the lessons they've learned along the way. Remember, we learn as much, if not more, from our failures as our successes. A willingness to share failures also helps to build trust.

Then stand back and watch what happens. Double down in areas where you seem to be gaining traction. Be alert to emerging unmet needs within the movement, and work to address them. Pursue every opportunity to help others achieve more impact and accelerate their learning.

Remember, the key to the success of movements is movement. Talking and theorizing is fine, but only if it leads to action. Action is helpful, but only if it is focused and directed toward a shared goal. The real power emerges when theory and action combine to change the world.

As you embark on this effort, focus on the following questions:

- **What are the biggest opportunities that could be unleashed by driving change in our existing environments?**
- **Who would be most motivated to address these opportunities?**

- **What call to action would be most effective in drawing these people together?**

- **Who might be enlisted to organize the initial cells in the movement?**

- **What early steps can be taken to connect these cells into broader networks?**

- **What key leverage points can we target in the relevant environment? That is, where can we get the most meaningful change in the shortest time with the least effort?**

CHAPTER 6

NARRATIVE ALIGNMENT

*Getting the Most Out
of Your Narratives*

Up until now, I've treated the four kinds of narratives as separate entities, but they can become deeply intertwined. When the narratives' creators do this in the right way, the intertwined narratives can significantly amplify and reinforce each other. But if they do it in the wrong way, their narratives can conflict with and undermine each other in ways that cause frustration and disappointment. Therefore, it is important to carefully avoid such misalignment.

This effort begins with our personal narrative. If we have not taken the effort to make it explicit, we'll have limited ability to productively shape the other levels of narratives. Once we have reflected on our own narrative, we are in a much better position to explore our context and tease out the other narratives shaping our surroundings. As I've suggested, narratives at all levels, with the notable exception of movement narratives, tend to be implicit, which makes them challenging to draw out. But the effort is worthwhile. When we look at the complex interplay across the levels of narrative, we can discover a lot of insights into what is helping us achieve impact and what might be holding us back.

One of the key roles of narrative is to provide leverage, helping us mobilize support from others, so we can accomplish together what we couldn't have achieved on our own. But if the narratives conflict with each other, we can feel isolated and undermined as the people around us are drawn in different directions. Alignment of narratives also enhances our ability to overcome the fear that more and more of us are feeling as we confront our rapidly changing world. Even if we can evolve our personal narrative to one that embraces opportunity, we may still be held back if the people in our institutions, geographies, and movements remain committed to threat-based narratives. As I've indicated before, emotions are contagious; we're much more likely to move beyond fear when we are in an environment that encourages us to do so.

Sometimes an institutional or geographical narrative can be the catalyst that convinces us to reassess and revise our personal narrative. As I mentioned earlier, this is what happened to me, though it took me quite a while to receive my wakeup call (I was 54). Once I took the time I needed to reflect, I realized I had been drawn to environments that supported a different narrative than the one I had been living.

My involvement in the antiwar and libertarian movements had exposed me to the cellular form of organization I now call creation spaces. I then found myself drawn to a geography, Silicon Valley, that fostered a culture of collaboration. Both showed me what can be accomplished when a shared opportunity-based narrative brings people together.

My journey through the institutional environment taught me a different set of lessons. My first job after graduate school was with the Boston Consulting Group, where I learned the importance of teams. Then I came to Silicon Valley to launch my startup. Scaling it and selling it to a much larger company taught me that having a shared goal drives more impact than simply adding people. I then had the opportunity to join Atari as a senior executive and discovered something less inspiring: success often breeds complacency. Atari had once been one of the fastest-growing companies in history; now it was just big. It taught me to never take success for granted. When I joined McKinsey & Company, I began to harness a different form of leverage. I discovered the power of pull—the ability to attract others who were also inspired by an opportunity out in the future and who amplified my efforts, even though we were not in the same institution and hadn't even known each other before. I started writing books framing opportunities that could inspire others to come together and to connect with me (and each other) as they embarked on efforts to address the opportunities.

But even as these movement, geographical, and institutional narratives were pulling me in one direction, I was still holding onto my fear-driven childhood narrative, which was all about addressing the needs of others on a one-to-one basis. My second divorce finally pushed me to reassess and reframe my personal narrative into a call to action to many people.

The broader narratives in the environments around me helped me change my personal narrative for the better, but they can just as easily confine and undermine our ability to achieve impact. Think about it. If the institutions and society around us don't value the opportunities we see, or if they cultivate practices that make it challenging for people to come together and collaborate, we're going to have a much harder time making our call to action succeed. Even more fundamentally, if the environments we live and work in are driven by threat-based narratives that reinforce and amplify our fears, then people in those environments will be skeptical of and resistant to the opportunities that excite us. We won't even realize these opportunities exist if we haven't bothered to articulate our personal narratives and sought to evolve them in ways that would help us achieve more of our potential. That's the starting point. But you shouldn't stop there.

Once you've articulated and evolved your personal narrative, start reflecting on your surroundings. What institutions do you participate in? What are their narratives? What communities do you live in? What are their narratives? Do these institutions and communities amplify the call to action that your personal narrative is framing for others? Or do they undermine the call to actiono? Are these institutions or communities supportive of the opportunity you are striving to address? In some cases, they may be hostile to the opportunity or, more broadly, hostile to *any* opportunity because they have embraced a threat-based narrative that intensifies fear.

If those broader narratives conflict with your personal narrative, then you have to do something about the conflict. In some cases, you might be able to help revise those broader narratives, so they become more consistent with your personal narrative. This is more likely to happen in smaller institutions or communities than in bigger ones, assuming you occupy a position of influence.

If you can't change the broader narratives, then you have to make some choices. You can either resign yourself to a life of frustration or decide to seek out institutions or communities whose narratives are more consistent with yours. That second choice can be very disruptive in the short term, but it could ultimately allow you to find people who will be much more receptive to your call to action. At a minimum, it is important to seek environments that are embracing opportunity-based narratives rather than threat-based ones.

Actually, you have a third choice. You also could start a movement that will seek to drive change in the institutions and communities around you. If you as an individual don't have enough influence to change those broader narratives, you can mobilize others to join you. If enough people can see and appreciate the opportunity for change, there is no limit to what can be achieved.

It all begins when you see the disconnect between your personal narrative and the broader narratives that surround you. To bring them into alignment you might have to target even bigger and more meaningful opportunities than you have in your personal narrative, or you might have to change your environment.

One client I worked with, an executive at a large oil company, told me he had become aware of how much his fear was controlling him and holding him back. We worked together to articulate the personal narrative that had been shaping his emotions and actions. He realized it was a threat-based narrative and began to look for ways to change it. What really motivated him, he realized, was the opportunity to develop alternative energy technologies that would be more sustainable and environmentally friendly.

As he began to focus on this opportunity and evolved his personal narrative, he realized how misaligned it was with where he worked. His company's institutional narrative was squarely focused on the threat of migration away from fossil fuels; it was staunchly opposed to the very things that excited him. His fellow executives were becoming increasingly fearful as they saw the mounting opposition to fossil fuels as a primary energy source. He could have quit, but after making a significant effort, he found an ally in a very senior executive who saw the advantage they could reap by investing in the development of alternative energy technologies. With that executive's support, he created an "edge" in the company with a charter to build and scale an alternative-energy business.

Although he was able to change his institution, the geography was a much harder nut to crack. He lived and worked in a city and country in the Middle East that were evolving threat-based narratives as they perceived increasing challenges to their traditional cultures in a rapidly changing world. The people around him were becoming increasingly driven by fear under the influence of these threat-based narratives. In an effort to better align his evolving opportunity-based narrative, he convinced his company to locate his edge initiative in Singapore, a city and country whose narrative was more opportunity based.

That was just the beginning. He has become involved in movements driven by the threat of climate change and is working to convince their leaders that they can have a much greater impact if they shift from threat-based narratives, which focus on the catastrophic implications of climate change, to opportunity-based ones that focus on the thriving ecosystems that can be fostered as a result of harnessing the potential of new technologies that reduce and capture carbon.

BOTTOM LINE

If you want to make the journey beyond fear, it's not enough just to look within yourself and reflect on your personal narrative. You also have to look around and determine whether the environments you live and work in are supportive of your goals. You have to decide whether their narratives support a call to action that can motivate others into joining your mission. Our environments significantly shape our ability to address big and inspiring opportunities. A major part of our journey involves finding or shaping environments that will amplify and reward our efforts, instead of holding us back. Most fundamentally, we need to find or evolve environments that embrace opportunity-based narratives rather than threat-based narratives that intensify the fear of those around us.

This applies to us as individuals, but it also applies to us in our roles as the leaders or employees of a business or any other kind of institution. Resist the temptation to be inward looking—a temptation that is that much stronger when we are driven by fear. Pay attention to the narratives of the geographies you operate in. Your institutional narratives will be a lot more effective if you are in geographies that have embraced opportunity-based narratives. Your success as an institution will be much more likely if you can help shape the narratives of the geographies you are in, so they also help people move beyond fear. If you are the leader of a business or institution, don't just focus on crafting an institutional narrative; explore its potential to be evolved into a movement narrative that creates a much deeper set of relationships with your key stakeholders.

Here are some questions to focus your efforts:

- **What are the narratives of the institutions, geographies, and movements that shape the environments where you live and work today?**

- **How supportive are these narratives of the personal narrative you are evolving?**

- **If your personal narrative is at odds with these broader narratives shaping your environment, can you influence the evolution of these broader narratives?**

- **If not, could you achieve much greater impact if you changed your environment by working with another institution, moving to another geography, or joining other movements?**

PART 2

THE PASSION OF THE EXPLORER

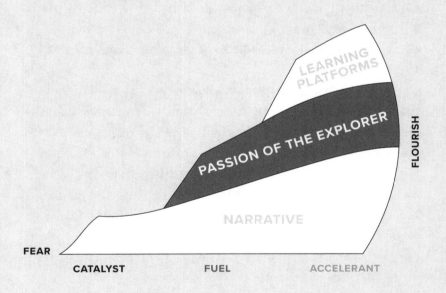

LEARNING PLATFORMS

PASSION OF THE EXPLORER

FLOURISH

NARRATIVE

FEAR

CATALYST   FUEL   ACCELERANT

I n this second part, I will explore how passion can unleash emotions that motivate us to take risk and move forward in spite of our fear. I focus on a very specific form of passion, which I call the "passion of the explorer," which emerged from research I have done. It is the second pillar, along with narratives and platforms, that can support us in our journey beyond fear. The first chapter in this section, Chapter 7, explains what I mean by passion of the explorer, how it differs from other forms of passion, why those differences are important, and how narratives can catalyze and unleash it.

The rest of the section focuses on how we can identify and develop the passion of the explorer in ourselves. Chapter 8 does a deeper dive into the approaches that we can use to identify it and draw it out. Chapter 9 then addresses an obstacle to doing so that many of us face, especially if we discover our passion later in our lives. It then suggests approaches that can help us integrate our passion with our profession. As you will see, I strongly believe we will be much more successful in overcoming our fear if we can find a way to make a living from our passion, rather than simply pursuing it as a hobby after hours or on weekends.

CHAPTER 7

WHY THE PASSION OF THE EXPLORER IS SO POWERFUL

About a decade ago, in an effort to discover ways to overcome performance pressure, I undertook a study of the environments in which people achieved the most extreme and sustained improvements in performance. The best way to address performance pressure, after all, is to improve continually and accelerate that performance improvement over time. I explored many different environments, including extreme sports like big-wave surfing, extreme skiing, and solo rock climbing, in which participants were constantly moving beyond what many had come to believe were the ultimate limits. I also ventured into online war game environments, like *World of Warcraft*, where if you make the wrong move, you die (virtually).

I found something interesting. Despite the tremendous diversity of their contexts, all the people who were pushing the performance envelope had one big thing in common: each had cultivated a very specific form of passion, a questing orientation that I called "the passion of the explorer." I define this as a drive to go where others have never ventured, to continually raise the bar of the possible.

Before we dive into to what the passion of the explorer is and how you can leverage it to move past your fear, it's important to distinguish passion from other emotional states that are often associated with it. Passion is in a category of its own. It should not be confused with those other states, not least because they often create fear instead of helping us move past it.

DON'T CONFUSE PASSION
WITH OBSESSION

Isn't there a dark side to passion? Can't passion degenerate into an obsession that consumes us and makes us lose sight of anything outside it? We've all heard cautionary tales about people who became so consumed by their passion that they lost their social standing, their meaningful relationships, and ultimately their minds as obsession gripped their every waking hour, crowding out everything else. Literature is full of such stories, as are the tabloids, from Captain Ahab's obsession with the white whale to last night's episode of *20/20*. It's no wonder many people fear passion.

To say that passion becomes obsession is to imply that obsession is simply a more passionate form of passion—too much of a good thing. But the passion of the explorer and obsession are differences of kind, not degree. In many ways, they are opposites.

This is much more than a matter of semantics; there are profound distinctions between the passion of the explorer and the emotions that drive obsession. Passionate explorers are committed to personal improvement in their quest to achieve more and more positive impact in the domains they have chosen. People with obsessions are seeking not to improve but to escape their very identities by losing themselves in external objects, whether they are collectibles, celebrities, a love object, or anything else that can define them. Passionate explorers are driven to overcome their personal limitations, while obsessives are seeking to escape their personal limitations.

What makes this distinction confusing is that passion and obsession can look a lot alike. Both are generated within and manifest in outward actions or pursuits, which can provide purpose and direction. Both motivate people to take risks, to make sacrifices, and to step outside conventional norms to achieve what they desire. Most importantly, passion and obsession burn within us irrespective of extrinsic encouragement or rewards. This can lead to what traditional institutions perceive to be subversive or rebellious behavior, driving passionate and obsessive people to the edges of organizations and society.

Those edges are where the crucial distinctions between passion and obsession become clear. The first significant difference between passion and obsession is the role free will plays in each disposition: passionate explorers fight their way willingly to the edge so they can pursue their passions more

THE JOURNEY BEYOND FEAR

freely, while obsessive people (at best) passively drift there or (at worst) are exiled there. The degree to which free will determines one's movement to the edge will greatly determine one's capacity to succeed in that challenging environment.

Passionate explorers find edges exciting because they have a rooted sense of self. Passion inspires creation, and creators have a strong and meaningful sense of identity, defined not by what they consume (which has little or false expressive potential) but by what they make (total self-expression). For example, people who are passionate about developing new energy technologies like solar energy identify themselves as innovators in solar technology.

When I say they have a "rooted sense of self," I don't mean to imply that their identity is fixed. On the contrary, as creators, passionate explorers are deeply invested in constant personal, professional, and creative growth. They are constantly seeking to develop and diversify their talents in order to keep their creations innovative and their passion dynamic, sustainable, and alive. Those innovators in solar technology are constantly evolving their identity based on their latest accomplishments in pushing the frontier of solar technology performance.

Through the challenge of creation and the innovative disposition demanded by the ever-shifting edge, passionate people expand their personal boundaries, helping them achieve their potential. Passion gives them the energy and motivation to work hard—and joyfully.

In contrast, obsessive people have a weak sense of identity, because they displace their sense of self into the object of their obsession. Consider, for example, the obsessed sports fan who can only talk about her team or the infatuated fan of a rock star who builds his life around the star's tours and tabloid coverage, even though he and the star never even meet. (This becomes a strange form of self-obsession, which is why obsessive tendencies are frequently associated with narcissism.) Far from the joyful effort and striving inspired by passion, obsession is a strategy of escape. In conflating their identity with their object of fascination, obsessives not only can forget their inner selves but also insulate themselves from the challenging world around them.

The obsessive person's focus is narrow because such a person is less interested in complex growth than singular direction. Obsessive personalities may be driven to create, but their lack of determination to grow as people constricts the scope of their creativity. Rather than realizing their potential, they restlessly search for ways to compensate for their sense of inadequacy.

It's no accident that we speak of an "object" of obsession but the "subject" of passion. Obsession tends toward highly specific focal points or goals, whereas passion is oriented toward networked, diversified spaces. Objects of obsession are often quite narrow—for example, using a specific photo-editing tool, developing enhancements to a specific product, or developing new art around a specific pop culture character or icon. Subjects of passion, in contrast, are broad—for example, using digital photography to explore new perspectives, innovating within a broader category of technology, or experimenting with a certain genre of pop culture. Given this broader focus, passionate people thrive on knowledge flows to stimulate innovation, achievement, and growth.

Because passionate people are driven to create as a way to grow and achieve their potential, they are constantly seeking

out others who share their passion in a quest for collaboration, friction, and inspiration. Because they have a strong
sense of self, passionate people are well equipped to form relationships. They present themselves in ways that invite trust:
they have little time for pretense and are willing to express
vulnerability in order to receive the help they need for achieving their own potential. Because they are passionate, they are
willing to share their own knowledge and experience when
they encounter someone who shares their passion. They are
also intensely curious, seeking to understand the other passionate people they encounter in order to better see where and
how they can collaborate to get better faster.

In contrast, obsessive people hide behind their objects of
obsession. They care most about those objects, not others or
even themselves. As a result, obsessive people are hard to get
to know and trust, because they exhibit minimal interest or
curiosity regarding the needs or feelings of others and share
little of themselves. One of the hallmarks of obsessive people
is a tendency to rant endlessly and often repetitively about the
same thing, rarely inviting commentary or reaction.

The key difference between the passion of the explorer
and obsession is fundamentally social: passion helps build
relationships, and obsession inhibits them. Passion draws
other people in; obsession pushes them away. Therefore, you
can differentiate between passion and obsession by asking
this question: Is the person developing richer and broader
relationships, or is the person undermining existing relationships and finding it difficult to form new ones?

Passion creates options, while obsession closes them.
Passion reaches outward, while obsession draws inward.
Passion positions us to pursue the opportunities created by

the Big Shift, while obsession makes us oblivious to the expanding opportunities around us.

DON'T CONFUSE PASSION WITH AMBITION

Many people equate passion with ambition. Once again, it's a question of semantics, but I would suggest a key distinction, at least when it comes to the passion of the explorer. People driven by ambition tend to be more focused on personal success and the extrinsic rewards that success provides—the higher salary and the more prestigious title. For the passionate explorer, it's enough to achieve a higher level of performance or create more value for others in the domain.

In their quest for those extrinsic rewards, ambitious people trumpet their strengths and talents to the people around them. Since they play to win, they hew closely to the rules of the game, rarely thinking outside the box. Passionate explorers, in contrast, are driven to challenge the rules when they see an opportunity to have an even greater impact by innovating. Ambitious people use the people around them as stepping-stones, while passionate explorers constantly reach out to the people around them and ask them for help. Passionate explorers build trust, while ambitious people arouse suspicion, because they are so clearly focused on their own advantage. Ultra-successful entrepreneurs like Jeff Bezos, Elon Musk, and Steve Jobs were clearly motivated by intrinsic rewards as well as the material rewards they ultimately accrued. All of them continued to learn, take risks, and wrestle with big challenges long after they had attained status, wealth, and the other external markers of success.

A TAXONOMY OF PASSION

So much for what passion is not. What is it? Many would say passion seems to be all about emotion, especially excitement; to be passionate is to be deeply excited about something or someone. The word is often used to mean the opposite of reason, which is the use of our intellect to understand something. For those who are deeply embedded in rationalistic cultures, that renders passion deeply suspect. In this view, passion is a distraction and can lead us to do irrational things, so we need to stay focused on reason and the mind, not letting our emotions get in our way.

I agree that passion is about emotion, but I would strongly challenge the view that passion always stands in opposition to reason and that it somehow undermines what we can achieve with it. In fact, I would argue that when we put passion and reason together, we can achieve much more than we can with reason alone. While I fully accept the power of reason (something that has shaped my life), the question the rationalists tend to dismiss or avoid is what motivates us to apply the power of reason to achieve new insights. Saying that reason motivates us to apply the power of reason is a tautology. What inspires and sustains the pursuits of the lover and the scientist alike is passion.

In fact, passion is many things. A long time ago, I developed a taxonomy of passion to help build a shared understanding of its different forms and to highlight what is distinctive about the passion of the explorer. My taxonomy of passion reveals some of the different types of passion. In classic consulting fashion, it's a two-by-two matrix, focusing on two key dimensions: improvement goal and time frame (see figure). These categories of passion are not hardwired. The boundaries can be fluid, and one form of passion can evolve into other forms over time.

Passion Matrix

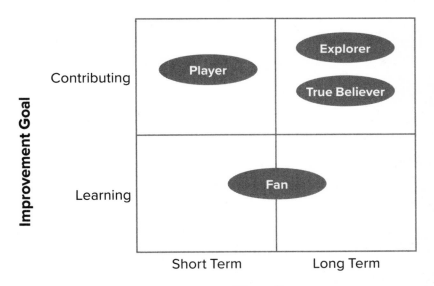

Along the vertical axis, we measure the improvement goal as being more about learning or contributing. Learning is finding out about the domain that is the subject of the passion, while contributing is about making a difference to that domain. The greater the passion, the greater the desire to leave the domain a better place than you found it. Of course, if your focus is on contributing, you are still driven to learn, but it's no longer learning for the sake of learning. Contributing leads to still more learning as you begin to see which efforts produce the largest impacts and which efforts produce the least.

The horizontal axis measures the time frame of commitment to the domain. A person can commit for just a short period, or there could be a long-term commitment.

As we explore these two dimensions, many different forms of passion emerge. Though I will have the most to say about the passion of the explorer, it's worth spending a little time on each form, since understanding the different kinds of passion helps us understand the unique potential of the passion of the explorer.

Passion of the Fan

Let's start with the passion of the fan. I've situated it in the lower half of the matrix, because for most fans, the passion is not about contributing to the domain so much as learning about it. We all know people with this kind of passion. They develop a deep interest in a person, team, idea, or discipline and set out on a quest to learn everything they can about it. Whenever they learn something, they get really excited, but their passion is insatiable; before long, they are off in pursuit of five new questions.

Fans generally seek each other out to ask each other questions and share what they've learned. There's never enough time to cover everything; conversations go on late into the night. If the passion is for a sports team, they go out of their way to see the team in action, even if it means traveling to distant cities. But when they go to the stadium, they stay in their seats; they don't want to go out on the field. Their passion is to learn about the players and the game. The only real contribution they want to make is to increase awareness of the domain for others, so that they too can become fans.

Passionate fans can be found in sports, music, theater, and virtually every other domain of knowledge or activity. For many years, I was a passionate fan of paleontology. I couldn't read enough books on the subject, and I had huge admiration for paleontologists like Mary Anning, Barnum Brown, Edward Drinker Cope, and Othniel Marsh. But I never once went out looking for fossils.

I've put the passion of the fan in the middle of the lower half of the matrix because it's not always clear how long the passion will last. With sports fans, the passion is generally long-lasting. Once they develop the passion, they're in it for decades. But others, like teens with the latest boy bands, become passionate fans for a period of time and then get bored and move on to something else.

Passion of the Player

If we move into the upper left quadrant of the matrix, we find a very different kind of passion, something I call the passion of the player. We've all met people with this kind of passion. They get deeply immersed in a topic or domain (or sometimes a person or a team) and not only want to learn more and more about it, but also are driven to create something or contribute something to the subject themselves, in a way that goes beyond mere conversation or discussion with other fans. They might want to pursue original research to discover some entirely new facts, write about the subject, build something, write fan fiction, or organize a fan club. In all these cases, the urge is to make a difference, not just learn about or talk about the subject.

Players can be fans who develop a motivation to create, as in the research of Henry Jenkins, a prominent media scholar who wrote about participatory cultures. Jenkins, in his book *Convergence Culture*, describes players coming together "to construct their own culture—fan fiction, artwork, costumes, music and videos—from content appropriated from mass media, reshaping it to serve their own needs and interests." Other examples of fans becoming players involve commercial products. Some fans of Lego building blocks become so passionate about this toy that they actively engage with the company on the design of next-generation products.

But there's a catch. Players have a hard time sustaining their commitment to a particular subject or domain. They get deep into it and make awesome contributions, but then they get distracted by something else and dive into that with equal vigor. This pattern repeats over and over again; nothing seems to hold them for very long.

Of course, some of these players do develop a long-term commitment to their domain. Their passion may evolve into the passion of the explorer. These categories of passion are not hard-wired. The boundaries can be fluid, and one form of passion can evolve into other forms over time.

Passion of the True Believer

As we move into the upper right quadrant of the matrix, we find a very different kind of passion: the passion of the true believer. True believers are deeply committed to achieving impact in a domain for the long term. They clearly see their destination in great detail and, perhaps even more importantly, the path they'll need to take to reach it.

The journey will be long and challenging but also an exciting, and true believers are committed to staying the course, doing whatever is necessary to accelerate movement down the path for themselves and for others. True believers work hard to draw others into their journey. But there's a catch. They cannot tolerate questions about either the destination or the path. These are a given, and to debate them would be simply a distraction and a waste of time. If you want to make the journey along the already-defined path, the true believer will welcome you with open arms. But if you ask uncomfortable questions, you'll quickly find yourself expelled from their inner circle.

Fundamentalist religions tend to cultivate the passion of the true believer, but true believers can be found in many domains. A lot of the entrepreneurs I run across in Silicon Valley and elsewhere are true believers. There are certainly true believers in large enterprises, schools, and governments as well.

Passion of the Explorer

I've saved the best for last—the passion of the explorer. People with the passion of the explorer bring together three elements. The first is a commitment to a domain, usually one that is broadly defined. They are excited about the prospect of having a growing impact in the domain over a long period of time, often a lifetime. That domain could take many forms. It might be an area of knowledge, like astronomy or sociology. It could be an industry or area of practice, like marketing or medicine or manufacturing. It could also be a geographic community or a craft, like gardening or woodworking. Whatever the domain, passionate explorers are not in it just to learn about it. They are committed to making more and more of an impact in the domain.

Here's a key difference between this type of passion and the passion of the true believer: Explorers do not have a detailed view of their ultimate destination but instead are inspired by a high-level view of an opportunity within it. Explorers also have little sense of the long-term path they will pursue. They are excited by the ability to evolve their own path as they go and the anticipation of their surprise and wonder when they find out where the path ultimately takes them.

A second characteristic of the passion of the explorer is what I call a questing disposition. It manifests when the explorer is confronted with unexpected challenges. Most of us dislike unexpected challenges, and many of us fear them. We want to get on with our plans and programs. Sometimes we ignore challenges in the hope they will go away if we wait long enough. Eventually, we find ways to work through them, but our goal is to get back to the activities we were already pursuing.

People with the passion of the explorer have a very different response: they get excited. They say to themselves, "Here's an opportunity to do something that hasn't been done before—to develop even more capability and have more impact than previously expected." What could be more exciting than that?

This questing disposition is a key factor in overcoming fear. When we meet a challenge we've never seen before, a very natural tendency is to be afraid. People with the passion of the explorer certainly experience fear when seeing a challenge for the first time, but they are motivated to move forward in spite of that fear. In fact, people with the passion of the explorer quickly get bored and frustrated if things get too easy. When that happens, they will often move to an environment where they will have more dragons to slay and can achieve more impact.

The third quality of the passion of the explorer is what I call a connecting disposition. Self-absorbed and individualistic as we often are, most of us tend to close ourselves off when we are confronted with a problem, retreating behind closed doors to figure out what to do. We reemerge when we've come up with an answer. Passionate explorers have a very different response. Their first instinct is to try to figure out who else might share their passion or have relevant expertise and ideas that can help them come up with a faster and better answer than they could on their own. As a result, they are constantly connecting with others.

One of the things I discovered as I studied people with the passion of the explorer is that they tend to come together in the creation spaces I described in Chapter 5. If you spend time with big-wave surfers, you'll find that they tend to have deep, trust-based relationships with a small group of other surfers who typically visit the same beaches on a regular basis. Similarly, players in online war games like *World of Warcraft* typically form small groups.

Passionate explorers build trust as quickly as they do because they don't put up a façade. They freely admit their vulnerability, which helps them move past fear. Think about it: when we try to solve problems on our own and fail, we often fall into a vicious cycle of defeat and self-loathing. We become trapped in our own heads and consequently become much more risk-averse. But if we can connect with others who share our excitement about addressing the challenge, we can move past our fear together.

Fitting Romance into the Matrix

You may think it's strange that I've written so much about passion without considering its romantic dimensions. Is there a place on the grid for the passion that arises in our relationships? There isn't, because truth be told, our passion for our partners can mimic many of the other types of passion I've discussed. There's the passion of the player, who avoids long-term commitments but has a deep desire to engage for a period of time. There's the passion of the fan, in which the goal is to learn as much as possible about the partner, but there is scant interest in helping the partner achieve more of his or her potential. There's the passion of true believers, who believe that they know their partner better than their partner does and that they know exactly what their partner should be doing to achieve their potential. Finally, there's the passion of the explorer—someone who is excited about the opportunity to learn more about their partner and to help them achieve more of their potential over time.

For those who believe that passion is experienced at the beginning of a relationship but then naturally dissipates over time, I recommend *Can Love Last?* by Stephen A. Mitchell, one of the most romantic books I have ever read. He argues convincingly that, by adopting the passion of the explorer (although he doesn't use this term), one can nurture and sustain passion in a relationship for a lifetime. The passion of the explorer doesn't just enrich our relationships with our partners; it can enrich all our relationships, including those with our children, our broader families, and our close friends.

The Importance of the Passion of the Explorer

The reason why the passion of the explorer is important goes back to the context for this book—mounting performance pressure and our natural human reaction to it, which is fear. Fear also has some predictable consequences: increasing risk aversion, shortened time horizons, adoption of a zero-sum view of the world, and eroding trust. These are all understandable but also dysfunctional. They pull us into a vicious cycle of increasing pressure and an increasing inability to respond to that pressure.

The passion of the explorer can change all that, helping us achieve far more of our potential by accelerating learning through action, which is a very different form of learning than reading a book or listening to a lecture. Focusing us on a long-term commitment to increase our impact in a specific domain, the passion of the explorer inspires us to constantly seek out new challenges as opportunities for development. It motivates us to connect with others and to foster growing networks of trust-based relationships. In short, it moves us from isolated passivity to collective action. Most importantly, it helps us move beyond our fear by drawing out hope and excitement.

PASSION AND REASON

While passion is a key to overcoming fear, we cannot fully leverage it without reason. Passion gives us agency by generating energy and a sense of freedom. Reason gives us needed structure by imposing constraint and discipline. Without structure, agency makes us an aimless whirlwind of activity, constantly distracted by the bright lights and unable to maintain forward movement. Without agency, structure makes us an inert mass, sinking deeper into the ground below, seeing the world but unable to explore it. In his classic book *The Prophet*, Kahlil Gibran put it eloquently:

> *Your reason and your passion are the rudder and the sails of your seafaring soul.*
> *If either your sails or your rudder be broken, you can but toss and drift, or else be held at a standstill in mid-seas.*
> *For reason, ruling alone, is a force confining; and passion, unattended, is a flame that burns to its own destruction.*
> *Therefore let your soul exalt your reason to the height of passion, that it may sing;*
> *And let it direct your passion with reason, that your passion may live through its own daily resurrection, and like the phoenix rise above its own ashes.*

Benjamin Franklin also expressed this sentiment more succinctly: "If passion drives you, let reason hold the reins."

We can gain more insights into the tight relationship between passion and reason by looking at five things that need to come together before we can achieve our full potential: focus, action, relationships, friction, and the framing of powerful questions and answers.

Focus

We need to be able to carve out specific domains we can focus on to achieve world-class performance. When we spread ourselves too thin, we risk being superficially engaged in too many areas to achieve world-class performance in any of them. But how do you pick the domain that offers the greatest opportunity to excel?

Passion provides the key. If you are not passionately engaged in a particular domain, you are unlikely to invest the effort and energy required to achieve mastery and distinctiveness. In his book *Outliers*, Malcolm Gladwell argues that successful people generally invest considerable effort over time—at least 10,000 hours—to master their domains. In a world of constant change, one could make the case that 10,000 hours is just table stakes; sustained excellence demands continued investment. It is very hard to sustain that kind of investment over years without passion to provide the motivation. If we rely solely on reason to select an appropriate domain, we may have a compelling logic, but logic alone is unlikely to sustain us as we begin to encounter obstacles and distractions and experience the fear of failure. Many people talk about the need for grit or discipline, but people with the passion of the explorer are excited about investing this time and effort to develop themselves. They don't have to force themselves to do it.

Once you have chosen a domain to focus on, reason provides a valuable way to frame questions and test the experiences you accumulate as you explore it. Reason helps you choose the most productive directions to pursue, and it helps you solve the difficult puzzles you will encounter.

Action

Having chosen your domain, you must engage with it and explore its furthest reaches (dare I say, edges?). It is not enough to sit in an easy chair and contemplate; you must roll up your sleeves and dig in to really experience the textures and particulars that give you the deepest insights into what is really going on.

Leaving that easy chair to venture into unknown territory presents real risks, and reason alone rarely helps us overcome our fears. In fact, it can deceive us into believing we can process information about the domain at a distance, keeping our attention focused on the forest, without the distraction of all those trees.

Passion will have none of that. It demands your full engagement and will settle for nothing less. It propels you forward, giving you the energy and courage to welcome any challenge as an opportunity to test yourself, regardless of the risk.

Once again, though, reason provides a welcome companion on the journey. It helps you reflect on your experiences and discern the patterns that emerge from seemingly random encounters. Reason allows you to see the themes that make the particulars less particular and part of a more coherent whole. It gives you powerful tools to make sense of rapidly evolving landscapes and to zero in on the underlying forces that drive and shape their evolution.

Relationships

To fully experience a domain, you must engage with people in ways that go much deeper than casual conversation and allow you to view things through different sets of lenses and build a shared understanding of the domain. Your shared passion helps you forge these important connections.

The passion of the explorer inherently drives us to connect with others. It provides capacity for empathy. It draws out the stories that are the first and often most powerful expressions of the new knowledge emerging on the fertile edges of your domain. Our research at the Center for the Edge showed a clear relationship between a worker's level of passion and degree of connection with others through a variety of avenues, including conferences and social media. Those who are motivated purely by reason are likely to find themselves less connected and therefore at a disadvantage relative to those who are connected through a shared passion.

At the same time, reason plays a role in forging and cementing bonds. A shared commitment to reason can help people overcome deep differences in experiences, assumptions, and perspectives. It can help build a shared understanding that offers access to the tacit knowledge each participant brings to the table. It also provides a powerful framework that lets you sift through idle distractions and zero in on what's truly relevant.

Productive Friction

Participants in the quest to achieve better outcomes should challenge each other. These challenges are productive friction when their intent is not to establish dominance or put each other down, but rather to create better outcomes, drawing upon a spirit of mutual respect and commitment to the quest. That spirit makes friction productive.

The passion of the explorer provides a fertile ground in which productive friction can emerge and flourish. Having a shared passion creates the trust that allows people from different backgrounds and experiences to engage with each other even when some of their most cherished assumptions are being called into question. Being on a shared quest to find the most creative ways to drive performance to new levels opens participants to new approaches that can deliver performance breakthroughs. If passion provides the context for fruitful debate, reason provides the toolkit needed to address and resolve differing views.

Framing Questions and Answers

Passion frames the most powerful questions, and reason frames the most convincing answers. This is another way to express the mutually reinforcing effects of passion and reason. As Claude Helvetius, a French philosopher during the Enlightenment, observes, "It is the strong passions alone that prompt men to the execution of . . . heroic actions, and give birth to those grand ideas, which are the astonishment and admiration of all ages." Helvetius gave one of the essays in his book *Essays on the Mind* the lengthy but pointed title "The Superiority of the Mind in Men of Strong Passions Above the Men of Sense." In it, he asserts, "It is, in effect, only a strong passion, which, being more perspicuous [sic] than good sense, can teach us to distinguish the extraordinary from the impossible, which men of sense are ever confounding; because, not being animated by strong passions, these sensible persons never rise above mediocrity."

In short, passion prompts us to ask the difficult and creative questions that "sensible" people would never think of asking. Framing the right question is one of the most powerful learning tools we have. With the right question, reason can help us generate powerful answers, but the question focuses the tool of reason and ultimately provides its power.

Reason and passion work together to overcome our fear of the unknown. Reason gives us confidence that we can handle any question, no matter how disturbing it might be. Passion provides the questions, setting in motion a virtuous cycle in which the better we get at wrestling with inspiring questions, the more we want to do it. As it plays out, our fear will naturally recede into the background, opening up a space in which we can become stronger and wiser.

TO FIND YOUR PASSION, YOU HAVE TO LOOK

If passion is so powerful, how do we find it and cultivate it? That is the focus of the next chapter, but for now, it is important to stress that the first important step is simply to decide to look for it.

Unfortunately, we live in cultures, societies, and institutions that conspire to discourage us from seeking our passion. We are regularly counseled to focus on acquiring skills that will be in high demand or to identify a natural talent we already have and choose a career in which it will be useful.

The unstated assumption is that we are at risk of not earning a decent living, so we need to focus on building our skills. Emotions are a distraction.

On the contrary, we need to understand that emotions are the key to our ability to achieve more of the things that matter to us the most. Fear is not a powerful motivator for learning. But when we are truly excited about something, we will be relentless in developing the skills and capabilities we need to succeed.

The key to discovering our own passion of the explorer is to pay attention to our emotions and the emotions of those we admire. We need to be relentless in our search for experiences that excite and inspire us, and we must not rest until we find the domain that generates the most excitement in us. We'll discuss this in more detail in the next chapter.

NARRATIVES AS CATALYSTS FOR THE PASSION OF THE EXPLORER

Narratives can be powerful tools for unleashing the passion of the explorer within us. The right narrative at the right time can create the conditions that catalyze and draw out the three attributes that define the passion of the explorer.

The right narrative draws out the first attribute—a long-term commitment to a domain—by helping us define domains and hear a call to action. Narratives are typically about a broad domain, rather than a narrow slice of experience, and tell about a big opportunity or threat somewhere in the future. Think about famous movement narratives like the ones that arise out of religions, national narratives like "the American dream," and regional narratives like Silicon Valley's. Consider institutional narratives like Apple's narrative about the opportunity to unleash our unique identity by harnessing new generations of technology and Nike's narrative about the opportunity to achieve exciting new levels of physical performance by moving from being passive observers to active participants in sports.

Besides mapping out a broad domain, a narrative calls us to make choices and take action, thereby moving us beyond simple curiosity to an active commitment to making a difference. An opportunity-based narrative identifies a wonderful opportunity within the domain that is available to all of us if we choose to pursue it. A narrative can provide a valuable focus for our efforts as we begin to explore a new domain. But ultimately, it's up to us. Will we make that commitment? Will we take the actions required to participate in that opportunity?

Opportunity-based narratives are not just about opportunities; they also frame the challenges we'll encounter along the way. To participate in the long-term opportunity, you need to take on and overcome the challenges that await you. That dual focus on opportunity and challenges helps to draw out the second attribute of the passion of the explorer, a questing disposition. Rather than trying to avoid challenges when they occur, narratives encourage us to seek them out.

Finally, to draw out the third attribute of the passion of the explorer, a connecting disposition, narratives assure us that the opportunity ahead is not just for one lucky winner. It's available to many, if not all, of us. These are not zero-sum opportunities. We can all participate and win. That message encourages us to come together to help each other over the finish line. The more people who share our excitement, the more excited we become.

As more and more people acquire the passion of the explorer, they accomplish awesome things. The stories of their amazing accomplishments begin to spread, giving additional credibility to the broader narrative. Look at what others have accomplished; you can do the same or even better. Will you join us? Will you make the choices and take the actions required to pursue this exciting opportunity? The narrative is enriched by the experiences of others. It spreads as more and more people see the tangible evidence of what can be accomplished.

Not all of us will be drawn equally to any one narrative. But narratives can become bright beacons that cause us to reflect on the purpose and direction of our lives. They are powerful antidotes to the institutions and practices that discourage and ultimately quash passion in their quest for predictability and standardization. They call us to reconnect with the passion we felt as children and to move from the passion of the player, which most of us had as kids, to the passion of the explorer, motivating us to make a long-term commitment to a specific domain.

If opportunity-based narratives can become a catalyst for drawing out the passion of the explorer, threat-based ones can do the opposite. You know the kind I'm talking about; we're increasingly surrounded by them. These focus on an imminent danger: we're under attack, and if we don't band together now, all the things we hold precious are going to disappear, and we'll probably die. Threat-based narratives are often deeply conservative or even reactionary. They want to preserve what we have, rather than explore what we could become. This tends to ignite a different form of passion—the passion of the true believer. In this kind of passion, the destination is clear, and the path we need to take to reach that destination is tightly mapped out. Threat-based narratives and the passion of the true believer have combined throughout history to create many of the social movements that have wreaked havoc in our world. Nevertheless, even here, the tight connection of narrative and passion helps to explain the power of these movements.

BOTTOM LINE

Passion can take many different forms. We can gain insight from stepping back and reflecting on whether we have developed any passions and, if so, what kind of passions we are pursuing.

We all need to find and cultivate the passion of the explorer. It provides the fuel that will sustain us on our journey toward whatever we are pursuing. Most importantly, it will help us overcome our fear and replace it with hope and excitement as we begin to address the expanding opportunities ahead. This is an imperative for all of us. We need to discover and cultivate the passion of the explorer that is within us all.

Narratives can be a significant catalyst in drawing out this passion of the explorer, helping to create a world in which pressure evolves from a source of fear to a source of excitement, calling us to achieve even more of our potential, both as individuals and collectively. By drawing out the passion that lies dormant within us, narratives can help us accomplish the seemingly impossible.

Some of us found the passion of the explorer early in our lives. Many of us are still searching for it, often unconsciously. If you are searching, certain steps ensure you will find it. I will tell you about those steps in the chapters to come. In the meantime, here are some questions for reflection:

- **Do you know anyone who has the passion of the explorer?**
- **Have you developed a passion of the explorer?**
- **If so, how might you connect with more people who share it?**
- **If not, are you actively searching to find a passion that engages you?**
- **If not, what has held you back?**

CHAPTER 8

FINDING YOUR PASSION

Some of us are lucky enough to have already found our passion of the explorer. Perhaps we came across a narrative that spoke to us deeply, igniting a flame within us. Or perhaps that flame was already lit, and we were inspired by how much brighter it made the world around us.

Many others are still looking, and many have given up hope, taking refuge in denial. We might acknowledge that others are capable of the passion of the explorer, but we have come to believe that this kind of passion is not for everyone. We have convinced ourselves that we're not capable of it, so it is futile to keep looking for it.

If you are one of the second group of people, I'm here to restore your hope. I felt that way once myself, but having experienced what can happen in my own life and seeing many friends and clients who thought they were doomed to a passionless existence learn otherwise, I've come to believe that all of us have the capacity to develop the passion of the explorer. It's just a matter of finding that passion.

WHAT HAPPENED TO OUR PASSION?

When I'm working with clients who are skeptical about the universality of passion, I ask them to go with me to a playground, so we can watch five- and six-year-old children playing together. Then I challenge them to find one child who's not passionately engaged in the exploration of the world—deeply curious, willing to confront challenges, take risks, and come together with their peers to discover more. Admittedly, most of the children are demonstrating the passion of the player, rather than the more fully developed passion of the explorer, but they all have a deep capacity for passion.

For adults no longer experiencing that passion, something happened to squash it: they went to school. Therefore, if we're serious about rediscovering and cultivating that passion, our first step is to overcome the skepticism and outright resistance to passion inculcated by the institutions that govern our lives, starting with our schools. With a few notable exceptions, teachers gave us messages to leave our passion at the door. When we were in the classroom, our job was to listen carefully, take good notes, memorize key facts and figures, and then play them back on our exams to prove we could follow instructions. If we have a passion, we were told, we can pursue it on the playground or after school.

Our schools aren't the only forces at work here. Many of us had parents who urged us to focus on acquiring the skills that offered the promise of lucrative careers or status in our communities. Many cultures around the world emphasize either material success or adherence to tradition as the pathways to fulfillment. These cultures view passion as an obstacle.

All of this prepares us for work environments in which the institutional model of scalable efficiency prevails. Rigidly regimented, these institutions are ambivalent about, even hostile to, any sign of passion among their workers. The key to success is to follow the process manual to the letter, executing tightly specified and highly standardized tasks predictably and reliably. I'm amused by the number of times I've heard executives say they want passionate workers, meaning they want people who will work nights and weekends on their assigned tasks. They certainly don't want anyone who will take risks or deviate from their scripts and potentially create an embarrassment. Once again, the message is that if you have a passion, feel free to pursue it after work as a hobby.

It's no accident that our school systems operate as they do. They were explicitly designed to take students who are not very well disciplined and teach them how to follow instructions, so they can do the same thing in the workplace after graduation.

Many of us give in to these institutional pressures. We learn that to get ahead, we need to suppress the passion within us. Some of us succeed so well that we forget we ever had the capacity for it. We've come to believe that, while some of us may be psychologically or genetically capable of passion, most of us just want to be provided with safe environments where we'll be generously compensated for performing our assigned tasks.

LOOK OUTSIDE

If we want to respond effectively to the pressures of the Big Shift, we have to defy those institutions and find the passion of the explorer, which we all have. If you are still in school or just starting to experience the world beyond school, you need to expand your horizons and venture out into many different domains to see if any of them spark the passion that lies deep within you. You need to resist the pressure to settle down and choose a life path based only on your parents' or community's expectations. The most important advice I gave my daughters when they were children was to seek out their passion and not stop until they discovered it. Even if we are older, we can benefit from looking outside, since so many of us fall prey to pressure to pick a path and stay on it.

LOOK WITHIN

We need to look within too, because when we reflect on our life experiences at different ages, we often see things in a new light. The passion of the explorer might be right there in front of us, just waiting to be discovered. It might not be fully developed, but we might see just enough of it that we can finally make it out, if we just take the time to look. Although younger people will have fewer experiences to reflect on, still they can and should look within. One of those experiences may offer a clue as to where their passion of the explorer resides.

Explore the Excitement

Start by looking back and recalling the most exciting times in your life. If nothing in school or your workplace excited you, what did you do for excitement when you had free time? What made those activities so exciting? While it may seem at first like there were many things, did they have any common elements that might provide some insight into the domain that triggers your passion?

When I first engaged in this exercise, I started to believe I had the passion of the player rather than the explorer. The things that had excited me throughout my life were so diverse that I didn't see a common thread. As I described earlier, the evolution of my personal narrative suggested I was drawn to promising edges that have the potential to change the lives of many others for the better. But that was too broad of an opportunity to be helpful. Was there a more specific opportunity that really excited me?

One of my earliest memories is of dragging my parents to construction sites on weekends and asking them to lift me onto the seats of the bulldozers parked there. I didn't want to play with construction toys; I wanted the real thing. I loved to imagine myself building offices where people would come to work. As I moved into high school, I became consumed by the study of the market dynamics that brought producers and consumers together, matching supply and demand in unexpected ways across great distances that were well beyond the capabilities of any of the participants to imagine in advance. As I continued into graduate school, I became excited by the discipline of business strategy—the ways companies could create much greater impact with far less resources when they understood the evolving structures of markets and industries. Then I discovered digital technology and the internet. I was mesmerized by its potential to augment human capabilities and connect people across the world in ways that would have been unimaginable a few decades earlier.

Talk about passion of the player! I was all over the map, from bulldozers to the internet, with many other stops along the way. I wasn't just interested in learning about these things; I was committed to making contributions to those domains, so I was definitely a player and not just a fan. But I had no long-term commitment to any one domain, or at least so I thought. Then I decided to step back and see if I could detect a common thread in those varying interests. That was a turning point.

I discovered that these interests did have something in common. What excited me was the concept of platforms that bring people together to accomplish what they could never accomplish on their own. It started with the buildings I imagined emerging from the construction sites of my childhood, and it continued to evolve until I encountered global digital infrastructures. These platforms didn't have to be physical; they could involve more abstract mechanisms like governance structures and protocols and standards—for example, market pricing mechanisms or strategic choices on where and how to play to best leverage your own and others' capabilities. The key to all of this was that something was bringing people together in structured ways to help them accomplish new things. That is what I was excited to explore.

As you reflect on what has excited you, don't just focus on your activities. Spend some time thinking about what you have read or seen that gave you real excitement. The science-fiction novels I read as a child were early indicators of my latent passion. What excited me the most about them was their descriptions of amazing technology platforms that brought people together to explore edges on earth and in outer space. My passion for science fiction was definitely the passion of the fan, but it gave me a clue to the passion of the explorer that was lurking within me, waiting to be discovered and nurtured.

Another opportunity for exploration is to reflect on the institutions and places that have excited you. As a child, I remember being very excited by our visits to Florence when we briefly lived in Italy. On reflection, what fascinated me was how Florence had been a magnet for so much talent and how those talented people had reinforced and amplified each other's creativity. I was drawn to Silicon Valley for the same reason.

While I didn't articulate it at the time, the geographical narratives those places had crafted spoke to the passion of the explorer within me. Both Renaissance Florence and Silicon Valley called people to venture out onto unexplored edges to achieve more of their potential and created geographical platforms that helped them come together.

As you explore the experiences in your life that have excited you, here are some questions to focus on:

- What was it about those experiences that excited you the most?

- If you had similar experiences over time, did they always produce excitement?

- If different kinds of experiences have excited you in your life, what common elements, if any, can you identify that all those experiences shared?

Reflect on the People

Another way of discovering your passion of the explorer is to reflect on the people you sought out over your life and with whom you have collaborated. When and where have you actively sought help from others? Over the years, who has amplified your energy, and who has drained it?

When I sat in those bulldozers as I child, I imagined I was surrounded by all the other people it took to build those awesome buildings. Later in life, I actively sought out people who were developing new insights and products and services in the unexplored edges I was drawn to. They were relatively few, but they were as excited as I was about the opportunity to make a unique contribution. Those were the people who amplified my energy. The people who drained me were the ones who wanted me to keep doing what I had already done, to stay in my comfort zone, not realizing that that zone was no longer comfortable for me.

As you reflect on what might be your passion of the explorer, consider the people you have admired throughout your life. Ask yourself why they inspired you.

In my case, it started with my parents. Even though I had a difficult childhood, I very much admired them. My father had hitchhiked from Pennsylvania to Peru upon graduating from college and found a job as a chemist with a mining company up in the Andes. During World War II, he went into the Amazon jungle in a quest to find more quinine for the US soldiers in the Pacific, who were suffering from malaria. He explored parts of the Amazon that had never been seen by outsiders and became friends with indigenous tribes. He truly was an explorer. I am convinced that is one of the reasons my mother was so attracted to him; she too had the drive to escape small-town America and explore the world. Talk about passion of the explorer! Both of my parents lived it, and I was deeply inspired by it.

Beyond my family, I had long admired architects—people like Frank Lloyd Wright and Renaissance masters like Filippo Brunelleschi. Later on, it was market economists like Ludwig von Mises and Friedrich von Hayek and business strategists like Michael Porter. More recently, it was digital tech pioneers like Steve Jobs, Doug Engelbart, and Tim Berners-Lee. All these people were edge explorers, venturing out into new frontiers and exploring ways that people could interact to accomplish more together.

As you reflect on the people who have inspired and excited you, here are some questions to focus on:

- What were the specific accomplishments of the people who inspired you?

- What domains were those accomplishments in? How broadly or narrowly might those domains be defined?

- What common elements across those accomplishments and domains might give you insight into what ultimately excited you about the impact these people achieved?

EVOLVE YOUR PERSONAL NARRATIVE

As I reflected on my experiences, I evolved a much richer personal narrative that explicitly leveraged my passion of the explorer. The narrative was no longer just about me helping others with their individual questions. It was a call to action that invited many people to come together and collaborate to achieve things we could not do on our own. It had a strong emotional component, which was something I had avoided before. I acknowledged the fear that those unexplored edges inspired, and I saw that when I ventured out to those edges with others who shared my passion, the fear became excitement.

Perhaps most importantly, my evolved personal narrative was much more explicitly focused on a domain, rather than just being an open-ended call for people who needed help. It was specifically a call to action to explore and address emerging opportunities for new kinds of platforms and ecosystems that could help people achieve more of their potential.

This is where it starts to get interesting. The people who respond to my call amplify my energy and intensify my passion, and the same thing happens with each of them. As our passion becomes clearer and brighter, more people respond, and a virtuous cycle is set firmly in motion.

In time, my new personal narrative led me to create a new institution (well, an institution within a much bigger institution) with its own institutional narrative—the Center for the Edge. It also led me to seek out other institutions with complementary narratives that help us achieve even more impact. I have joined the faculty of Singularity University, an institution focused on understanding and harnessing the potential of exponential digital technology to create a world of greater abundance for all. On another front, I joined the board of trustees of the Santa Fe Institute, which created a cross-disciplinary platform for academics from many institutions and disciplines who are exploring the dynamics of complex adaptive systems.

As a result of these and other efforts, I have developed a rich network of relationships that help all of us achieve more and more impact. And as I will discuss later, I am embarking on an effort to create a new platform that will help people make the journey beyond fear.

As you seek to evolve your own personal narrative, here are some questions to focus on:

- What is the most exciting opportunity in the domain that has become the focus of your passion of the explorer?

- Who could be most helpful to you in addressing this opportunity?

- What would motivate them to invest significant time and effort in helping you address this opportunity?

- What specific call to action will mobilize the people who can be most helpful to you?

BOTTOM LINE

Most of us have still not found our passion of the explorer. Many of us have even given up looking for it. Resist that temptation. The passion of the explorer is patiently waiting to be discovered, surfaced, and nurtured within all of us.

The search can be challenging and sometimes even frustrating. But it is worthwhile. It will require you to step back and reflect regularly to discover what really excites you. While much of this reflection needs to be done on our own, I have come to believe that we can also benefit from engaging with others as we pursue this reflection. Having people who know us is helpful, and sometimes complete strangers ask us hard questions. It is particularly helpful to connect with others who are on a similar journey to discover their passion of the explorer.

When we do find our passion of the explorer, we can use it as a powerful fuel to evolve our personal narratives in ways that will help us achieve even more impact and connect in much richer ways with those around us.

Until we have achieved a deeper understanding of what motivates us, how can we possibly expect to motivate others? But when our call to action is fueled by the passion of the explorer, it will be so convincing that it will help others discover their own great passion.

As you reflect on the passion of the explorer, here are some questions that can help:

- **Have you connected with your passion of the explorer?**

- **If you have, does your personal narrative capture the opportunity that is most exciting to you? Is it helping you connect with others so you can achieve even more impact in addressing that opportunity?**

- **If you haven't, are you investing the time and effort required to discover the domain that has the greatest potential to motivate you to achieve more and more impact because the excitement is irresistible?**

CHAPTER 9

INTEGRATING PASSION AND PROFESSION

Searching for your passion of the explorer will help you achieve far more of your potential, so it's worth doing well. You can greatly increase your potential for impact if you find a way to integrate your passion into the way you earn your living. This effort tends to run into resistance; as the previous chapter noted, organizations want dedicated workers but are rarely set up to benefit from creative people pursuing their passion of the explorer. However, as this chapter will show, we have some options for overcoming that resistance.

THE IMPERATIVE AND THE CHALLENGE

The Big Shift has been reshaping the business landscape for the past several decades, expanding opportunities while also intensifying pressure in the workplace, leading to stress, fear, and the risk of burnout. Without the passion of the explorer, we won't be able to muster the creativity and persistence necessary to address those opportunities.

To avoid that risk and address that opportunity, we need to integrate our passion and our profession, something few of us have been able to do thus far. At the Center for the Edge, we conducted a detailed survey of the US workforce and found that only 14 percent of workers experience the passion of the explorer in their jobs.

Despite more and more talk about the need for "lifelong learning," we hear very little about where the motivation to learn is supposed to come from. The unstated assumption appears to be that it is fear: if we don't add to our skills and knowledge, we will lose our jobs. True, fear can prompt us to do some learning, but those of us who have the passion of the explorer do not view learning as a burden. Instead, we actively embrace it, especially when we can gain new knowledge through working with others.

Unfortunately, the vast majority of us work for institutions that are wary of edges and deeply suspicious of the passions that draw people to explore them. One of the biggest reasons why only 14 percent of the US workforce has the passion of the explorer is that employers actively work to suppress it. That even those few have the passion is a tribute to their success in suppressing this emotion.

We were taught to think of our work as the price we must pay for the material resources needed for enjoying the rest of our lives. Our work environments were carefully designed to deliver scalable efficiency; there was no place for passion in them, we were told. Passionate people do not follow standardized scripts well. They are constantly improvising, challenging conventional wisdom, and striking out on new and unexpected paths. Passionate people are unpredictable; they take risks. They also detest the organizational politics that pervade their institutions, as leaders jealously protect their power and hoard resources.

Very few institutions measure the passion of their workforce. Instead, they are consumed by the concept of worker engagement. While definitions of worker engagement vary quite a bit, they generally focus on three elements: Do the workers enjoy the work they do? Do they like the people they work with? Do they respect the company or institution that they work for?

The evidence that engaged workers perform at a higher level than workers who are not engaged is irrefutable. But is engagement enough? Engagement as conventionally defined does not include a commitment to achieving higher and higher levels of impact over time. In this era of mounting performance pressure, such a commitment is an imperative. And that commitment is precisely what passionate explorers pursue.

There is another reason why worker engagement may be a misleading metric. Think about engaged workers who enjoy the work they are doing, and then imagine that you will now tell them their work must fundamentally change, given the new developments in the marketplace and the world at large. What is their reaction likely to be? For many, it will be resistance. They'll want to hold onto the work they enjoy so much. Passionate explorers, in contrast, welcome change. In fact, they actively seek it out because they view it as an opportunity to develop new capabilities and have even more impact.

SMALL STEPS TO CONSIDER

Given the degree of institutional resistance to passion, how can you find a way to integrate your passion with your profession? You start by taking some small steps. Reflect on your existing work and see if you can find elements in it that excite you. Then see if you can identify opportunities to evolve your work to build on them. If you work for a large institution, for example, do opportunities that would more effectively align with your passion exist in other parts of the organization? Suppose you work in the sales department, while your passion is much more aligned with marketing. Perhaps you could find a way to shift into that part of the organization.

A woman I worked with found herself in exactly this position. She had been a successful salesperson for a large automobile company but found the transactional approach of sales to be limiting. She had begun to see patterns of unmet needs and was excited about the opportunity to design and deliver marketing programs that would address those needs. As she gained more insight into the passion of the explorer, she was moved to find a way to pursue this opportunity. She reached out to senior marketing executives in her company and eventually found one who was intrigued by the opportunity she had identified and, more importantly, by the passion she displayed in her conversations about it. That executive shifted her into his department as one of his direct reports. Her efforts have achieved significant success. More importantly, she is now excited about going into work every day.

Another key is to seek out others within the institution who may share your passion of the explorer, so you can support and reinforce each other on your quests. Admittedly, there are likely to be very few, given the statistics I've cited, but there are some. The challenge is to find them.

Because of institutional resistance, those people are usually well hidden, pursuing their passion when no one is looking. Don't look for them in the core of the enterprise, in the most traditional jobs. Instead, they are likely to be in some newer part of the organization or in a distant branch office, where they have more freedom to pursue their passion. If possible, try to organize a small impact group of similarly motivated people so you can reinforce and multiply each other's impact.

Depending on the specific domain your passion focuses on, you may need to look outside the institution where you work. You may have ended up where you are because of accident, necessity, or social pressure—say, your parents convinced you that the only way to be successful was to become a lawyer. If that's the case, you might be able to start doing something in your spare time that is more aligned with your passion but also generates income. Perhaps you're already doing something you're passionate about, like woodworking or writing, as a hobby. Is there an opportunity to start generating some income by selling the products or services generated by your passion? This could become a path to your transition.

Ultimately, aligning your passion and profession may require looking for a new job in a new company, starting your own business, or moving to a different geographic region. That certainly will take an effort and pose a significant risk, but the rewards are likely to make it worthwhile. Take some time to reflect on the implications of staying in an institution that provides no outlet for your passion and demands more and more from you in areas you do not find fulfilling. Yes, you may be under a lot of short-term pressure to make a living, but you are likely to be even more successful when you find work that aligns with your passion.

A remarkable example on this front is a client I worked with who was a senior administrator at one of the leading universities in the United States. While very successful at a relatively young age, he was troubled by the fact that he found his work boring. He was intrigued by my notion of the passion of the explorer and asked me if I could help him find his. As we worked together, he realized that what excited him the most was fixing appliances. Since he had been a child, he had loved taking things apart and putting them back together. He loved the challenge of diagnosing problems and, most importantly, finding ways to repair them. As prestigious and highly paid as his administrative work was, it mostly involved processing endless paperwork, which drained him of all his spirit and energy. He couldn't wait for the end of the workday.

Before long, he decided to change his life. To the astonishment of his colleagues and everyone else in his life who didn't know him well, he quit his high-powered job at the university and set up an independent business as a handyman. He suffered a significant reduction in income in the short term, but his passion brought him great success. Word spread about the fix-it man who never gave up on a problem, and before long, so many people were calling him that he had to turn away some jobs. The last time we spoke, he told me he was looking to hire people to help him. Drawing on the lessons he had learned, he was determined to hire only people who shared his passion. He didn't want to hire someone who just needed a job.

I've been on this journey myself. Early on, I decided to accumulate as many academic credentials as I could. My parents paid a significant price for that, for which I am eternally grateful. But I also paid a significant nonmonetary price by enduring years of "education" that required me to go through endless classes and courses. Fortunately, I was able to skip most of the classes, read the assigned texts, and demonstrate that I had memorized the relevant material.

Once I graduated, I resolved to find a profession that would align with my passion. I actually turned down an opportunity that would have paid me millions as a very young man, because I found the work to be uninteresting. Over the next couple of decades, I shifted back and forth between start-ups and large management consulting firms. At the startups, the process of taking a business concept and working with others to make it a reality was deeply satisfying but also totally consuming. In those jobs, I lost any perspective on the rest of the business world and my personal life. The upside of consulting was that it exposed me to a wide range of business problems and people that stimulated and challenged me. I was stimulated by the fact that I could never predict what the next day would bring. I was torn between these two sets of experiences—startups and management consulting.

It took me a while, but I finally realized that the best way to integrate my passion with my profession was to do something entrepreneurial within a larger management consulting firm. While I was at McKinsey & Company, I helped to launch the firm's office in Silicon Valley, and I launched two consulting practices within the firm. Years later, when I was asked if I would be interested in setting up a new research center at Deloitte, I jumped at the opportunity, not least because it gave me a chance to explore new kinds of institutional platforms.

The journey continues. Writing this book has been a catalyst for me to imagine a new platform—something I call an *activation center.* While I will continue to research the journey beyond fear, my more important goal is to develop programs and platforms that will support people in making the journey beyond fear and help to evolve institutions that encourage and reward that journey. This will integrate a different form of consulting (perhaps better described as coaching) with a bold entrepreneurial effort to become a catalyst for a much broader movement to redesign our institutions so they become places that nurture the passion of the explorer.

DRIVING CHANGE FROM WITHIN THE INSTITUTION

While some people may have to do more soul searching to discover a company and a role that aligns with their passion, some of us are lucky enough to already work in a company within our domain. Your issue might be that the work you're doing isn't as well aligned with your passion as it could be or that your institution's leaders are insufficiently supportive. In that case, you should consider focusing on driving change within your institution.

Even those who have discovered their passion of the explorer and pursued a career that integrates it are often unhappy in their jobs, frustrated by the obstacles they encounter at every turn. They see all the possibilities but experience the barriers that keep them far out of reach. Well-meaning mentors advise them to get with the program and embrace the institutional agenda, even if it means leaving their passion at the door every morning. These people are naturally frustrated that what should be their biggest asset is viewed as a threat.

Rather than just tolerating the prejudices of our institutions, we need to issue a call to action within them, catalyzing and driving efforts to transform them into places that don't merely tolerate the passion of the explorer but actively foster it. Ultimately, that may be the best way to integrate our passion and our profession.

While this battle can seem overwhelming in the short term, we can draw hope and inspiration from one inescapable fact: one way or the other, our current institutional homes have to change. Performance pressures will continue mounting, driven by the broad deployment of new technology infrastructures and public-policy trends that are reducing barriers to entry and movement. If they don't change, they will fall by the wayside as a new generation of institutions specifically designed to address those unprecedented opportunities emerges.

I mentioned in the Introduction the 75 percent decline in return on assets that US public corporations have experienced over the past five decades. That trend provides compelling quantitative evidence that current approaches to scalable efficiency are no longer working and are leading to diminishing performance over time. Unmet needs are staying unmet; new ways to create value and accelerate performance improvement are not being deployed. Passionate workers are powerful catalysts for institutional transformation, whether they remain within the institution or serve outside its boundaries, operating on its peripheries in various roles.

Given the new infrastructures that are emerging, we have an unprecedented opportunity to engage in a new form of innovation: institutional innovation. Product and process innovation are still valuable, but they are inevitably limited in scope and potential as long as organizations pursue them within existing institutional arrangements.

To thrive and draw others into our camp, people with the passion of the explorer need to rethink whole institutional architectures—the roles and relationships that define how institutions function. Instead of pursuing scalable efficiency, institutions must learn how to pursue scalable learning. In other words, they must make talent development and performance improvement (getting better faster) the core rationale for their existence. Everything about these institutions—strategy, operations, and organization—must be reconceived through this talent development lens. As these efforts to craft a new set of institutional arrangements advance, we passionate explorers will move from the edges of institutions to their cores.

To be clear, when I refer to scalable learning, I am not talking about learning as a process of sharing existing knowledge. The most valuable form of learning is the creation of new knowledge. The best way to pursue it is through action, so you can observe the impact and learn through objective experience. What matters is impact. The best way to address unseen problems and opportunities for value creation is to mobilize small but diverse groups that are committed to accelerating impact. This requires a very different form of organization.

Shifting from an institutional model of scalable efficiency to one driven by scalable learning will require grueling efforts. If we don't undertake them, the scope of our learning and our impact will be constrained. Properly configured, institutions can provide extraordinary platforms to amplify and accelerate our individual efforts. We can still make a difference without them, but it will be far more contained.

Our existing institutions are largely helpless to participate in the growth opportunities emerging at their edges, where unmet needs and emerging new technologies create unexploited opportunities. Yet they must redeploy more and more of their resources from their cores into those unexplored white spaces on the edges of their enterprises if they are going to survive. We can lead them, from the outside in.

The initiatives we develop on those edges may take many forms. Some may address the needs of a small but rapidly growing segment of customers who could ultimately dominate the market. Some may address a broader set of emerging needs of a larger set of existing customers. Some will be driven by the emergence of new technologies that enable creation of far more value at much lower cost.

To drive the transformation of the institution, these efforts must have the potential to scale to the point where they become the organization's new core, rather than simply being a set of diversification or growth initiatives. And to achieve the potential of transforming the core, the initiative to scale the edge must gain the support of at least one very senior executive, ideally the CEO or someone who reports to the CEO. That senior executive will need to have the commitment and courage to resist efforts to squash the edge initiative and preserve the core as it is.

The people at the edges will be more receptive to the necessary changes and will be the first to master the new practices that will drive those changes. Many of us may be using the new practices already, albeit in a limited and fragmented way. As we continue to engage on the edge, we will be applying these techniques in much more systematic and creative ways. Our growing impact will position us to draw more and more resources out of the core. New institutional forms will evolve and scale rapidly, enhanced by a new set of individual practices that make passionate workers even more successful.

To accomplish all of this, we explorers will need to find each other and join forces to expand our impact. The march ahead of us will be long and hard, but all we have to lose are our institutional chains. The path is clear: we have the opportunity to move from passion to profession and finally potential.

To achieve this, we need all the leverage we can mobilize. New developments like the Creative Commons, open-source software, innovative approaches to motorcycle design in China, and the impact groups that drive performance in extreme sports are early indicators of the opportunities ahead. But imagine what could be accomplished if we mobilized the vast resources already residing within our existing institutions.

We need to move forward and engage them, and those institutions need to listen to us. Twentieth-century institutions are not succeeding in the twenty-first century as new digital infrastructures take hold. They must change, or they will slowly shrink into shadows of what they once were.

Make no mistake, the institutions will marshal significant resistance to each and all of the fundamental changes they must make. I have long warned my clients of the power of the immune systems within large institutions. The antibodies they can martial are deadly efficient—and it's no wonder, since people's livelihoods, ways of life, and identities are at stake. Their reactions are understandable; these are well-intentioned people who believe they are doing the right thing. Nevertheless, they are ultimately driven by fear and must not be allowed to prevail. Instead, we need to find ways to overcome their fear and move them to hope and excitement.

We must remember that fear feeds fear. A burning-platform message ("If we don't change, we'll all die!") just feeds the fear and hence the dysfunction. The more frightened people are, the more desperately they'll hang onto what made them successful in the past, and the harder they will resist any efforts to change. Ultimately, however, what motivates people to embrace risk and pursue really big opportunities is not fear but hope and excitement.

With the right effort, we can turn our institutions from prisons to powerful learning platforms and achieve the potential we have long dreamed about, both for ourselves as individuals and for the institutions that support us. Once we have done this, we will finally have aligned passion and profession at scale.

INSTITUTIONS BENEFIT AS WELL

Throughout most of this chapter, I have focused on our needs as individuals. Individuals can achieve much greater impact in the domains that excite them when they can devote more time to them, and they are likely to be much more successful in their work if they are truly passionate about it.

But individuals aren't the only beneficiaries. Imagine what our institutions could accomplish if all their people were driven to continually increase their impact, instead of simply putting in the hours and collecting a paycheck. In this world of mounting performance pressure, institutions that cultivate passion gain significant competitive advantages.

Although few institutions are tracking the passion of their employees, much less seeking ways to cultivate it, this can change. One of my favorite examples of a company that worked to unleash its employees' passion is Toyota, which redefined the work of its assembly line workers. It told them they had some routine tasks they had to do—they were on an assembly line, after all—but their real job was to identify the problems that emerged in the course of their work and then not just file problem reports, but immediately fix the problem they spotted. If they couldn't fix a problem themselves, they were to pull a cord next to their workstation, and the company would swarm them with a team of experts. They would be heroes for finding a problem that needed to be addressed.

Passion levels of workers on the assembly line soared, because instead of just doing routine tasks that anyone could do, they were identifying opportunities to become more productive and achieve more and more impact. While certainly not everyone could become passionate about working on an automobile assembly line, this example suggests that institutions can redefine work in ways that draw out more potential from their employees, and in doing so, they benefit their bottom lines. Sadly, the opportunity is mostly untapped.

BOTTOM LINE

Once we have discovered our passion of the explorer, we need to align it with our work. While we can try to do that individually, we're likely to have much greater impact if we work together to transform our institutions, leading them from the edges. This is not just an imperative that we should pursue out of fear, but a huge opportunity.

Here are some questions to consider:

- **If you have discovered your passion of the explorer:**
  - **Is your job providing you with an opportunity to pursue this passion at work? If so:**
    - > **Have you been able to connect with others at work who share your passion of the explorer?**
    - > **Is there anything you can do to help transform the institution you work for so it can cultivate your passion more effectively?**
  - **If your job is not providing an opportunity to pursue this passion:**
    - > **Are there ways you can evolve your job so that it focuses more on your passion?**
    - > **Are there other job opportunities within the institution that would be more aligned with your passion?**
    - > **Is there anything you can do to help transform the institution you work for so it can cultivate the passion of the explorer more effectively?**
    - > **Would you be better able to pursue your passion by finding another institution to work for or perhaps even launching a startup?**
- **If you have not yet discovered your passion of the explorer, are you aggressively searching to find that passion, as discussed in the previous chapter?**

PART 3

THE ROLE OF LEARNING PLATFORMS

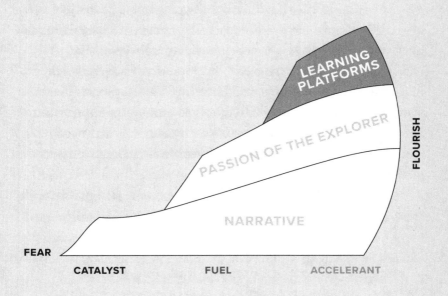

n this last part of the book, I will explore the role of learning plat-forms, the third pillar of positive emotion, along with narratives and the passion of the explorer. Various kinds of platforms exist in our economy and society, but I am focused on a specific kind: learning platforms. They are an invaluable tool that can help us on our journey beyond fear.

In Chapter 10, I will define platforms in general and identify four kinds of platforms. Then I will explain why I believe that learning platforms can be powerful in helping us overcome fear and cultivate the passion of the explorer. The short answer is that they harness the network effects that drive exponential improvements in impact as more and more people come together to learn faster.

Chapter 11 dives deeper into the untapped potential of learning platforms. It also explores the design elements required to scale them successfully.

By helping us come together and collaborate with others who share our excitement and hope, learning platforms accelerate the impact of opportunity-based narratives and the passion of the explorer, unleashing exponentially expanding opportunities.

CHAPTER 10

THE PULL OF PLATFORMS

Achieving More Together

So far, this book has explored the roles of opportunity-based narratives and the passion of the explorer in helping us move from fear to hope and excitement, amplifying our impact and accelerating our learning and performance improvement. Both pillars are powerful on their own, and in combination, they can help us get better even faster. The third pillar, which amplifies our impact even more, is platforms.

Today the word *platform* appears in many contexts. Platforms are still in their earliest stages of evolution, so as great as their impact has already been, we should be careful not to narrow our horizons. There's much more to come, but we're going to need to seek it out. Let's begin with a definition.

WHAT ARE PLATFORMS?

The word *platform* is used so loosely that it can mean virtually anything. A platform can be a physical object to stand on, a declaration of principles (as in a political platform), a type of shoe sole, a metaphorical platform representing an opportunity for discourse, or a computer platform combining a variety of technology layers. Here, I am focusing on platforms that help people to come together and interact with each other. For our purposes, it means two things: a governance structure and a set of protocols and standards for interaction. The governance structure specifies who participates, what roles they play, how they interact, and how disputes get resolved. The protocols and standards help facilitate connection, coordination, and collaboration among a growing number of participants. For example, a retail platform specifies what requirements a vendor must meet in order to participate and the requirements that must be met in order for a transaction to occur. It will also specify standards regarding how products are presented and protocols for how prospects can interact with vendors when considering something to purchase.

Too many of us today think of platforms as a subset of technology without looking deeper to discover what makes that technology so helpful. Platform technology can help in scaling platforms (just look at the incredible reach of social media, such as Facebook, Twitter, TikTok, and Reddit), but it is only an enabler. The key is to focus on *what* platforms enable.

The power of platforms is their ability to support the interactions among a growing number of participants. We can interact with each other in family units and small groups, but when we want to expand our interactions and impact, the process gets complicated. How do we do that in a way that serves the needs of individual participants and the broader group as a whole?

As discussed earlier, virtually all institutions have evolved a model of scalable efficiency. Think of multinational corporations or the governments of large countries like the United States or China, with their complex organizational charts and vast bureaucracies. Scalable efficiency operates by tightly specifying all activities, assigning them to specific people, and then carefully monitoring those people to make certain the activities are performed reliably and efficiently. Accomplishing this requires a large amount of administrative overhead, which necessarily constricts the scope of what can be done.

Platforms offer a different approach. As mentioned, they provide a governance structure and high-level protocols and standards to facilitate interactions, but they generally leave it up to the participants to determine what kinds of interactions they will have. This requires far less administrative overhead and can be scaled with much less cost and complexity. For example, LinkedIn provides guidelines for people to form groups on its platforms but then leaves it up to the moderator of the group to establish high-level policies on what topics participants can discuss in the group.

DON'T LOSE SIGHT OF THE ECOSYSTEMS

In contrast to institutions, with their chains of command and performance management systems, the platform approach requires us to be much more aware of the needs of the participants and to ensure the platform facilitates interactions that participants will value. Therefore, people who want to use platforms should understand the broader concept of ecosystems, specifically human ecosystems, because they can help us accomplish what we need or want or they can hinder us.

We are all deeply enmeshed in a complex set of human ecosystems. For the purpose of this discussion, let me define a human ecosystem as the set of interactions and relationships that emerge and evolve among independent participants as they come together in communities and organizations. Some ecosystems are intentional—for example, a movement or political system set up to bring people together. In other cases, they are more spontaneous and emergent, like a city that draws people to live there. In actual practice, all ecosystems tend to foster a blend of intentional and spontaneous interactions that evolve over time

Like many other terms that have gained broad usage, *ecosystem* is used very loosely, so it can create a lot of confusion. Are all ecosystems created equal? What are the differences among them, and why might one choose to participate in one type of ecosystem and not others? At the Center for the Edge, we identified twelve types of intentional ecosystems and explored their differing structures and the relative advantages that each one has in particular contexts. We will focus here on the interactions that bring people together across more than one institution so they can experience and accomplish more than they could within a single institution.

An example of an intentional ecosystem that extends beyond a single institution is the collection of specialized independent providers that large construction firms assemble so they can have the right expertise at the right time to support specific projects. Another example would be the supply chain of a large industrial company—for example, makers of parts, suppliers of raw materials, providers of transportation services, and warehouse operators. Each participant in the supply chain has an assigned task, which it performs on an ongoing basis to support the manufacture, assembly, and distribution of certain products.

THE ROLE OF PLATFORMS IN ECOSYSTEMS

For ecosystems to scale, they need governance structures, standards, and protocols to facilitate interactions among their participants. This is what platforms can deliver. The governance structure specifies the procedures people must follow to resolve disagreements, for example, and, for extreme cases, the offenses that merit expulsion from the ecosystem and the procedures that might be necessary to expel someone.

Standards and protocols help the participants communicate with each other and support specific forms of interactions. For a transaction like purchasing a product, how do we ensure proper recordkeeping and accurate billing? For giving access to a database, how do we identify users and protect their private information? Answering these questions requires an ability to anticipate the kinds of interactions that are likely to emerge within the ecosystem. Will the platform just support conversations, or will exchanges of goods and services occur? New kinds of interactions may emerge, so healthy ecosystems support the ability to evolve their governance structures, standards, and protocols as participants gain insight into what their changing needs might be.

For example, eBay initially addressed the interests and needs of hobbyists and collectors who were excited to generate some income from their activities; it helped them connect with customers. Over time, it emerged that some vendors were challenged by their lack of business experience. In response, eBay evolved the ecosystem to allow members to support each other in providing advice and coaching on what is required to build a profitable and sustainable business.

Platforms provide support for ecosystems to scale and evolve, but they do not need to be supported by digital technology. In fact, until the last few decades, they were not. For millennia, the basic elements of platforms were not even written down. They were expressed as shared beliefs or norms about how people should interact with each other, passed down verbally from generation to generation and evolving as the needs of the participants evolved. If the norms didn't evolve, they often withered and died as they became less useful.

Today, of course, digital technology platforms are increasingly important for allowing ecosystems to grow. With the internet and more and more affordable digital technology, platforms have the potential to reach anyone. Anytime and anywhere, the members can interact in any number of ways and carry out complex transactions. By saying technology isn't necessary, I mean to emphasize the importance of not getting so distracted by the technology that you fail to focus on the reason the platform exists, which is to support the ecosystem and the interactions that fuel it. Without those, the platforms are hollow shells, as MySpace became when Facebook stole its thunder.

Platforms' ability to scale ecosystems is especially important when we consider one of the most powerful attributes of ecosystems: network effects. The concept of network effects is relatively new but familiar to many of us. It says that the more participants who join an ecosystem, the more valuable it becomes to each participant. For example, if there's a marketplace with only one product for sale, it is of minimal value, but the value rapidly grows as more and more products become available and as more and more customers join the ecosystem. The value created by network effects often increases exponentially, not just linearly. The bigger and faster a platform can scale an ecosystem, the greater its exponentially increased value, and the sooner that value can be reaped.

A lot of the value in ecosystems and platforms comes from the power of pull. Pull can involve greater ability to draw in people and resources. Certainly, the ability to access talent and material resources when you need them is very powerful. Two other, often neglected forms of pull are the ability to attract (pulling in people we didn't even know existed) and the ability to pull more and more of our potential out of us as we interact with a larger number of people.

A TAXONOMY OF PLATFORMS

To understand the untapped potential of platforms, let's start by comparing four distinct types: aggregation, social, mobilization, and learning platforms. I'll briefly describe all four. In the next chapter, we'll do a deeper dive into the category I believe is the most significant untapped opportunity in the platform world: learning platforms.

Aggregation Platforms

The platforms familiar to most people today are aggregation platforms. These platforms bring together a broad array of resources and help their users connect with those resources. They tend to be focused on transactions or tasks, such as buying shoes or looking up research articles. The key is to express a need, get a response, do the deal, and move on. Aggregation platforms also tend to operate on a hub-and-spoke model, meaning that all the transactions are brokered by the platform owner and organizer.

Within the category of aggregation platforms are three subcategories:

- **Information aggregation platforms.** These include stock performance databases for investors and scientific databases for researchers.

- **Marketplace and broker platforms.** These provide an environment in which vendors can connect with customers, usually anytime and anyplace. Popular examples are eBay, Amazon, and the iPhone App Store. In a growing number of cases, these platforms draw out resources that were previously not available. For example, by encouraging people to make spare rooms in their homes available to travelers, Airbnb has created a platform that grew more than tenfold, from 50,000 to 550,000 listings in less than four years, creating a market that rivals the traditional hospitality industry. In fact, it was strong enough to have a successful initial public offering in late 2020, at the height of the pandemic, when tourism was at its nadir.

- **Contest or crowdsourcing platforms.** On these, someone can post a problem or challenge and offer a reward or payment to the participant who comes up with the best solution. Two examples are InnoCentive or Kaggle.

Aggregation platforms can help people pursue their passion and their opportunity-based narratives by giving them greater ability to access helpful services. With the right features, aggregation platforms can allow participants to attract resources they weren't even aware of.

Social Platforms

Social platforms, which are the second most common form of platform available today, resemble aggregation platforms in that they aggregate a lot of people. Think of all the broad-based social platforms we've come to know and love: Facebook and Twitter are leading examples. The pull of these platforms is irresistible to many. US adult users spend an average of 42.1 minutes per day on Facebook and 17.1 minutes on Twitter; some spend much more.

Social platforms differ from aggregation platforms on some key dimensions. First, they build and reinforce long-term relationships across participants on the platform; it's not just about doing a transaction or a task but getting to know people around areas of common interest. Second, they tend to foster mesh networks of relationships, rather than hub-and-spoke interactions. In other words, people connect with each other over time in more diverse ways, and these interactions usually do not involve the platform organizer or owner.

As we have seen, pursuing your passion of the explorer and your personal narrative motivates you to connect with others, which helps you overcome fear and builds your excitement and hope. Social platforms can help in this quest, but the next two types of platforms can have much greater impact.

Mobilization Platforms

A mobilization platform takes common interests to the level of action. Users don't just have conversations about common interests on these platforms; they focus on moving people to act together to achieve a shared outcome beyond the capabilities of any individual participant. Because of the need for collaborative action over time, they tend to foster longer-term relationships, but the key focus is not social but results oriented. The aim is to connect with a group of people and put them into motion.

Many different kinds of mobilization platforms exist. In a business context, the most common is a "process network" platform, which brings together participants in extended business processes like supply networks or distribution operations. A prime example is Li & Fung, the global sourcing company in the apparel business; many others span a wide variety of industries, including motorcycles, diesel motors, financial services, and consumer electronics. A little further afield—because they are not profit-making enterprises—are Wikipedia and open-source software platforms like Linux or Apache. Even further afield are mobilization platforms that support social movements, such as in the Arab Spring movement.

A mobilization platform is especially useful to those pursuing their passion and personal narrative, because it is explicitly designed to help people come together to achieve some common outcome. But the next category we will consider is even more powerful for supporting us in our journey beyond fear.

Learning Platforms

Learning platforms help their users learn through action by giving them a forum for sharing their initiatives and publicly reflecting on what went right and what didn't. These platforms aren't just aggregation platforms to support learning. An aggregation platform can support learning by bringing together resources like online video courses or by providing access to information in databases or catalogs. Those aggregation platforms certainly can help participants learn, but the effort is largely an individual one. In contrast, learning platforms as I describe them are built on the belief that we can learn faster by acting together than we can by simply reading or listening to a lecture by ourselves. Learning platforms enable us to solve problems and discover best practices via the power of crowdsourcing.

Very few examples of learning platforms exist in business, but we can find large-scale learning platforms in arenas as diverse as online war games (for example, *World of Warcraft*) and online platforms to help musicians develop and refine their remixing skills (for example, ccMixter). They have also emerged in a broad array of extreme-sports arenas, including big-wave surfing and extreme skiing.

Ultimately, learning platforms can have the greatest impact in supporting us as we craft our narratives and nurture our passion. An important driver of our fear is our sense that the world is changing in ways that require us to learn faster. Learning platforms can help us reduce this fear while equipping us to have more and more impact in the domains that excite us.

THE BUSINESS MODELS THAT SUPPORT PLATFORMS

In a world where more and more of our interactions are shaped by large-scale commercial platforms, we have to ask an important question: Who pays? Creating and maintaining a platform requires resources, which means a viable platform needs a business model, such as funding the platform with advertising or charging people a fee to participate.

While platforms are designed to support the needs of the participants, the practical reality is that the needs of some participants often outweigh the needs of others. Typically, the needs of the participants who are paying the bills will get priority over the needs of the rest who are using the platform but not helping to cover its costs. Many of the largest and best-known platforms today are supported by advertising revenues, so the needs and interests of the advertisers often get more attention than the users' needs and interests.

It's ironic that advertising, a key component of the push-based mindset and practices, has become the dominant business model for commercial platforms whose focus is on helping participants pull rather than push. In the push-based marketing model, advertisers intercept us wherever they can and push their messages at us, trying to motivate us to buy their products. In the pull-based marketing model, vendors try to be so helpful to their customers and users that word will spread and more and more people will seek them out.

An open question is whether this advertising-supported business model will prevail as new platforms emerge and existing platforms grow and evolve to serve a broader range of needs. I suspect that, as we evolve beyond today's aggregation and social platforms to focus more on emerging needs around mobilization and learning, we may begin to see more direct-payment models, in which all the participants help to fund the platform's operation.

While subscription models are an easy default, the platforms most likely to succeed in the future will be more flexible. A relatively easy first step would be to charge based on usage. An even better model might be one where participants pay based on value received. Of course, the challenge is to be able to measure and monitor the value received, but it would be a catalyst for the platform owner and the participants to reflect on what is the most meaningful value the platform can deliver.

Also relevant to business models is that, as platforms seek to address our mobilization and learning needs, trust will increase in importance. Before we will share the kinds of feelings and needs these initiatives require, we'll need to be convinced that the platform owner is really committed to serving our interests. Convincing us becomes much more challenging when advertisers are paying the bill. Trust in many of the best-known platforms is already eroding as we learn how much of the information we share about ourselves is being sold to third parties—a very different form of learning than is provided to the platforms' users. Ultimately, the platforms' success will depend on how well their owners can align their own interests with those of all the participants on their platform.

If the platforms' business models erode trust and promote conflicting interests, we will use them only in very limited ways—say, to do quick transactions or to share family photographs with networks of "friends." If we are convinced that our interests and the interests of the platform owner are aligned, we'll use them to build the deep relationships that will help us in our quest to address opportunities.

CONNECTING PLATFORMS WITH NARRATIVES AND PASSION

How do platforms tie into opportunity-based narratives? Aggregation platforms support opportunity-based initiatives with information and resources, and social platforms can be helpful for finding and connecting with potential participants. But platforms will get really interesting when they are specifically designed to mobilize participants to learn faster as they work toward a common goal, doing things that have never been done before. As we will see in the next chapter, mobilization and learning platforms have not yet been widely deployed, even though the need for them is growing and they offer almost limitless potential for making the journey beyond fear.

While we wait and prepare for learning platforms, even aggregation and social platforms can help to harness a second level of pull: attraction. As I suggested earlier, when most of us use these platforms, we focus on the first level of pull, which is access. When we are looking for specific information, products, or people, we use the platforms' search mechanisms to find what we need.

However, those of us who are pursuing the passion of the explorer are much more likely to see the benefits that platforms can provide from attraction—that is, pulling in people who you didn't even know existed but who can be extremely helpful. That requires you to ask for help, which is hard to do when you're trapped in a world of scalable efficiency, in which you need to project as much strength as possible. To show your vulnerability is to reveal your weakness to people who might exploit it, so you talk about your accomplishments instead. People who have embraced an opportunity-based narrative know they can't pursue their quest without help. But without that narrative and that passion to motivate us, we're much less likely to tap into that second level of pull.

Of course, there are ways to use existing platforms to drive attraction, but it's a very different kind of attraction and one with much more limited value. I call it the attraction of the insecure, and in our world of mounting performance pressure, more and more of us are likely to feel it. We post cute pictures of our pets or amazing vistas from the latest trip we made. We're not really interested in attracting people to us who understand our needs and are motivated to help us. We just want to be reassured that we're worthy of attention. But that attention is fleeting and distracting; it's not an enduring and effective response. If anything, it makes us even more vulnerable over time as we realize how fleeting and meaningless it is.

To harness the third level of pull—achieving more of our potential by drawing out capabilities within us—we gain strength and direction from combining platforms with opportunity-based narratives and the passion of the explorer. The most helpful platforms for this are learning platforms, and we will learn more about them in the next chapter.

BOTTOM LINE

As powerful as opportunity-based narratives and the passion of the explorer are, their impact can be significantly enhanced by platforms. The platforms that exist today can be helpful, but the ones that could help most—learning platforms—have yet to achieve their full potential.

Even with the platforms that are available now, you can begin to tap into the power of platforms. To help you determine how, here are some questions you might want to reflect on:

- **On which platforms do you spend most of your time?**
- **Which platforms have helped you achieve more of your potential?**
- **How have you gotten the most value from using these platforms?**
- **How could you use those platforms to further enhance your network of personal relationships and achieve even more of your potential?**

CHAPTER 11

ADDRESSING THE UNTAPPED POTENTIAL OF LEARNING PLATFORMS

Many people are talking about platforms, but hardly anyone is talking about learning platforms. It's a big white space that could play a major role in unleashing our full potential.

As I suggested in the previous chapter, the primary objective of learning platforms is to help users learn faster together through action, feedback, and reflection, enabling them to evolve their practices over time to achieve more and more impact. True, other platforms also have learning potential. Aggregation platforms connect us with information, resources, and people that can answer our specific questions. Social platforms allow us to learn about people. And on mobilization platforms, we learn what works and what doesn't work as we seek to achieve certain goals. But the learning that occurs on these other platforms is a by-product, not the platforms' primary design goal.

THE DISTINCTIVE VALUE OF LEARNING PLATFORMS

In a world of mounting performance pressure, we need to move beyond "learning about" to "learning to do," and from there to "learning to do better and better." Once we venture into this territory, we need to find ways to learn together. No matter how smart any of us are individually, we'll be a lot more creative and effective if we come together with others who are motivated to achieve more and more impact.

If we don't find ways to do this, we'll become increasingly stressed and marginalized. Not only is pressure mounting, but the rate at which the world is evolving is accelerating, so anything we learn today may become obsolete tomorrow. That means learning must be both lifelong and faster.

Consequently, platforms will become more and more central to our survival, much less our success, because they have a unique capability to accelerate learning. In the previous chapter, I mentioned platforms' network effects. When more participants join a platform, its value increases exponentially. That happens even if none of the participants are learning. They can simply connect with more resources to meet their specific needs of the moment.

With learning platforms, a second order of network effects comes into play. These platforms go beyond increasing value by offering a growing range of choices. In addition, the more participants who join the platform, the greater and greater the diversity of experience, expertise, and perspectives everyone can tap into, so participants can learn faster. This second order of network effects ultimately has the greatest value and potential for exponential improvement. In fact, the ability to connect with a growing range of static resources has diminishing value in a rapidly changing world. We need to find environments where everyone is getting better faster.

Of the three levels of the power of pull that platforms can help unleash, I've so far focused on two: access and attract. The third level, achieve, provides the greatest impact. Achieve is about finding ways to activate more of our potential and pull it out of us. That comes from learning through action.

If we're not learning, we won't activate our potential; it will remain dormant. We have to make a conscious effort to pull it out of ourselves, and then we'll make an amazing discovery: our potential is unlimited. The more potential we pull out of ourselves and apply in the world, the more we will find to tap. But to do that, we need help from learning platforms. Without them, we can never take full advantage of this third and most powerful level of pull.

HARNESSING THE VALUE OF LEARNING PLATFORMS

Here's a key point: learning platforms offer only the potential to learn. To harness that potential, the participants have to be motivated. If we're not motivated to learn, we'll view learning as a burden rather than an asset.

Many of us would still like to believe that all that effort we invested in learning in the past was sufficient and that we are now entitled to simply reap its returns. Learning requires time and effort. In a world of mounting pressure, it's natural to view that effort as just one more form of pressure to be avoided at all costs.

That's where narrative and passion come into the picture. Without these two critical pillars, we're unlikely to develop the motivation we need to take full advantage of learning platforms as they evolve. With these pillars, we experience an insatiable demand to learn faster together.

Once we have crafted or embraced an opportunity-based narrative, we are highly motivated to come together with others to achieve it. We are increasingly aware of the obstacles and roadblocks that stand in our way, challenging us to find creative new ways to overcome them. To meet the challenge, we need to learn why these obstacles are so challenging. We're not going to figure that out on the first try; we will likely experience many failures along the way. But each failure is an opportunity to learn and find even more effective ways of moving forward. Learning is the key to progress.

When we have found and cultivated the passion of the explorer, we are committed to making an increasing impact in our chosen domain, so that it becomes a better and better place. To do that, we look for the challenges that goad us to achieve something new. We actively seek out others who can help us overcome the challenges. We are driven to learn together through action.

Each of the pillars of positive emotion can exist in isolation, but the goal is to bring all three of them together. People who are inspired by an opportunity-based narrative will often discover the passion of the explorer. Similarly, people with the passion of the explorer are often inspired by a large opportunity they see in their domain. When these two pillars come together, watch out! People who are driven by both passion and narrative to learn faster together are unstoppable. As they pursue a way to do so, they will catalyze the growth and evolution of learning platforms.

As they emerge and evolve, a powerful virtuous cycle will come into play. The availability of platforms that make learning easier and more fulfilling will inspire some of their users to discover their passion and evolve their narrative. As more and more of these inspired people become active on these platforms, the platforms will evolve to become more helpful to them, better serving their need to learn faster together. That will inspire still more people to find their passion and their narrative, and the cycle will become unstoppable.

KEY ATTRIBUTES OF EFFECTIVE LEARNING PLATFORMS

Perhaps the central design element and benefit of a learning platform is that it enables participants to create shared workspaces in which they come together in small groups, build trust-based relationships, and collaborate on initiatives. This brings us back to the concept of creation spaces, which I introduced in Chapter 5 in the context of movements. Creation spaces are present in successful social and political movements throughout history, as well as environments in which we see sustained extreme performance improvement, like extreme sports and online war games. Although these environments are diverse, participants have evolved very similar ways of organizing to learn faster together to achieve more impact. The basic unit of organization is a small group, typically consisting of three to fifteen members, who meet frequently to work on initiatives designed to achieve local impact. These impact groups then link together in an ever-expanding network of cells that can learn from each other and leverage each other's efforts.

As the need to accelerate learning continues to unfold, impact groups will become the core unit of organization in every aspect of our lives—our personal growth efforts, our work environments, our communities, and the movements that will drive change in the world. We will need platforms that are more explicitly designed to support both the impact groups and the larger networks of groups.

In addition to providing the shared workspaces where groups convene and collaborate, the platforms can help scale the groups' efforts by providing features enabling greater collaboration. These would likely include broader discussion forums, in which participants can direct their questions to the members of other groups, combined with directories that can help participants across the entire platform find each other based on their relevant experience or skill sets. Besides asking questions, forum participants can share stories about the initiatives they have already undertaken, describing what worked, what didn't, and what key lessons they took away from the experiences.

Especially as these initiatives start to have more impact, they can inspire other participants to make even greater efforts. Feedback loops are key to learning through action, but if you don't know what impact you achieved, it's hard to assess whether your action was effective and what you might need to change. Therefore, learning platforms should provide a systematic way to measure and track performance, so participants can explicitly see the impact they are achieving.

Learning platforms could further enhance learning by framing and staging challenges for participants when they join. A precedent for this comes from online game designers, who are careful to stage challenges in a way that draws in players and motivates them to seek higher and higher levels of performance. As soon as a player successfully meets a challenge, another challenge invites them to rise to another level. In many gaming platforms, most players can meet the early challenges without help from others, but as the challenges progress, the incentive to collaborate increases. On learning platforms, the early challenges should follow a similar pattern. They should be neither so easy they seem trivial nor so difficult they discourage participants.

Another delicate balance involves the degree to which the platform structures participation. The platform should be neither too open ended nor too prescriptive. A structure that focuses participants on the opportunities and challenges that really matter can be helpful. However, the platform must also leave space in which participants can come up with new approaches themselves. Some of the most powerful learning occurs when we see something that no one else had thought of. Such an insight can lead to a totally different set of approaches, perhaps with far more impact.

Of course, diversity of thought also can lead to conflict, so platform organizers and the groups that form on the platform need to evolve governance structures. These should be explicit about what is permissible and what would be grounds for exclusion from the platform, leaving as much room as possible for divergent approaches. The balance is necessary, because as I've mentioned before, productive friction can accelerate learning and performance improvement. Learning platforms need to foster environments that encourage participants to challenge each other in a spirit of mutual respect, believing that everyone's contribution is potentially important.

Many, if not all, of these features are already embedded in environments I have discussed in earlier chapters—successful movements, extreme sports, and online war games. With the exception of online war games, however, we have yet to see all these features fully developed online. While I have nothing against war games (I was, after all, an executive at Atari), I am eager to see more learning platforms that can help us achieve real-world impact. An opportunity-based narrative may be inspiring, and the passion of the explorer may be highly motivating, but both will do far more to help us achieve our potential if they are supported by scalable learning platforms that can bring together people from all over the world.

OPPORTUNITIES FOR EXISTING PLATFORMS

While there is a big opportunity for a new generation of platforms that can address this unmet need, existing platforms have potential to evolve in ways that help participants learn faster if platform developers add the necessary features. If existing platforms don't evolve in such ways, most will be overtaken by the inevitable new entrants.

To begin, platform developers must cultivate a richer understanding of the ecosystems they were designed to support. Their participants' needs are evolving, and platforms must anticipate the new needs and meet them head-on. None of the features of an ideal learning platform are beyond the reach of existing platforms.

For example, many platforms already include a reputation profile, which can help participants assess each other's credibility. A participant's reputation profile might include testimonials from those who have interacted with the participant, identifying the value they received from the interaction. This is a key to building more trust, which is essential for collaborative learning and performance improvement.

Also, many platforms today host discussion forums, which could develop into shared workspaces. Effective discussion moderators can provoke more fruitful dialogues by drawing in more participants and helping to keep the conversation focused on the topics at hand while preserving the ability to fork a discussion into adjacent topics or subtopics. This is one of the most badly needed skill sets in online discussion forums; it can make the difference between a meandering conversation and a real learning experience. (I wrote about it extensively in my book *Net Gain* more than twenty years ago, but it's still a major gap.) Online discussions would add even more value if the platform more effectively archives them and makes them searchable, so later participants can benefit from them.

Going a step beyond moderation, platforms could provide coaching. Learning is not just about conversation. Platform providers could train coaches to help emerging impact groups identify actions they might take, monitor their effectiveness, and help them reflect on how they might achieve even greater impact in the future.

Another feature that many existing platforms could add or refine is the opportunity to define and implement performance feedback loops. Inviting participants to identify the performance that matters to them and helping them measure their performance could significantly help the learning process.

AN EARLY PLATFORM
FOR LEARNING

Many years ago, enterprise software developer SAP created an online forum for application developers responsible for writing applications to access and leverage SAP programs. Since then, it has evolved remarkably in support of learning.

SAP invited application developers who'd run into problems when writing code to post questions and see if anyone else had encountered a similar problem and could suggest how to address it. Participation didn't require a lot of effort. The user simply had to frame and post the problem, and no one was expected to spend hours figuring out solutions. The hope was that if someone happened to have already found one, they would share it.

This proved to be such an attractive environment for application developers that over two million of them participated in the forum. As a result, when a developer posted a problem, a satisfactory solution was often posted in a matter of minutes. The productivity of SAP's application developers significantly improved.

One feature that made participation more attractive to the developers was a reputation profile, which awarded points

for offering workable solutions. The more solutions participants offered, the more points they received. The reputation
profile also recorded the expertise demonstrated when a
solution was provided so that users had objective benchmarks
to assess each other's credibility. That catalyzed something
unexpected. Participants built reputation profiles in certain
domains, and then other participants began to seek them out.
In other words, the interactions expanded beyond problems to
solve. These participants wanted to exchange ideas with people sharing their expertise and interests. The forums evolved
into a much richer set of discussions that were sustained over
time and helped the developers learn from each other.

Something else started to happen, too. Application
developers who shared the same interests and ideas began to
collaborate in developing entirely new applications. As SAP
observed this, it began to provide shared virtual workspaces
in which these new development teams could come together.
Interestingly, the team members were often geographically
distant from one another. If not for the SAP platform, they
might never have found each other. As these collaborative
efforts began to unfold, an entirely new level of learning
was unleashed: now the developers were learning together
through action, rather than just conversation.

A PRACTICAL STARTING POINT: MINIMUM VIABLE PLATFORMS

The SAP example underscores an important point that is
often missed by platform developers and will be particularly
important as platforms evolve. The single biggest cause of

failure in platform initiatives is to try to do too much too soon. When technologists design these platforms, they fall prey to the temptation to include in the initial release all the bells and whistles they can imagine will be needed. The problem is that the people designing the product are often not very good at anticipating what the participants' real needs will be. In fact, such a platform's complexity can scare away potential users who are not yet convinced of the platform's value.

A far better approach is to start with the concept of a minimum viable platform. That concept asks, "What is the narrowest group of participants who can be targeted at the outset, and what is their most pressing need?" Then you focus on getting a platform deployed that addresses it. Next, you work on getting a critical mass of participants to experience that need being met, so word of the platform's value will start to spread. (Everyone talks about the network effects of platforms, often forgetting that those network effects don't kick in until a critical mass of participants has joined. Until then, platforms have the "empty bar" problem: people enter but can't find what they were looking for, so they leave, never to return.)

When a critical mass does begin to assemble, you watch how the participants use the platform. What features and functions don't they use? Consider getting rid of those. What are participants looking for and not finding? Add new features to the platform to address those unmet needs, as SAP did.

My favorite example of the power of staging—which wasn't an intentional staging effort—comes from Facebook's early days. Remember, it started as a platform for the students of one school, Harvard University. Out of all the possible reasons why students would want to connect with each other,

Facebook's early success was in helping students connect based on attractiveness ratings. That enabled it to reach critical mass quickly. Only then did it expand its reach to students at other Ivy League universities, then at all universities, then at high schools as well as colleges, and eventually to anyone 13 and older.

THE CHALLENGE OF LEARNING PLATFORMS

Developing and evolving learning platforms will involve some significant challenges. One arises because success breeds complacency. Some of the most successful businesses today are platform businesses, but the existing platforms are firmly wedded to the model of either an aggregation platform or a social platform, and they show little inclination to address this untapped need. They are also heavily dependent on an advertising or commission-based business model that tends to favor the interests of certain participants over others. This undermines the trust that is a key building block for learning, but moving away from that business model could prove very challenging.

A broader challenge is one that confronts most of our institutions today. Virtually all of them are firmly wedded to the scalable-efficiency institutional model. That model is deeply suspicious of platforms in general and tends to underestimate the learning imperative. That is because scalable efficiency is ultimately a command-and-control model: the most reliable way to get efficiency at scale is to tightly control all the people and resources required to deliver value. To the extent that this model acknowledges a need for learning, the tendency is to want to bring the necessary expertise and capability in-house. That's also one of the reasons that we are seeing a growth in M&A activity globally and a widespread trend toward reducing the number of participants in supply chains and distribution channels. The fewer participants outside our organization that we have to depend on, the more assured we can be of getting the results we need, especially when we are focused on cutting costs rather than increasing the value we deliver to our customers and other stakeholders.

Platforms, however, make us more and more dependent on others for the resources we need, so they are perceived as undermining control. When institutions couple the perceived loss of control with a lack of appreciation for the ability and need to learn faster by collaborating with others who have different skill sets and perspectives, learning platforms seem risky and impractical.

The prevailing mindset and culture will need to shift dramatically before our institutions can reap the benefits of learning platforms. The catalyst for making that shift may have to be us, acting as individuals. We too are experiencing performance pressure and similarly want to tighten control over our surroundings. Wherever possible, we want to become self-sufficient and less reliant on others.

But that could change as the passion of the explorer helps us turn pressure into opportunity. As we begin to see what others who already have this passion are accomplishing and how motivated they are to achieve even more, more and more of us will search for and find that passion within ourselves. The connecting disposition of this passion will motivate us to overcome our fear and seek out others who share our passion, so we can work together. Our openness to collaboration will increase still further if we are fortunate enough to encounter an opportunity-based narrative that shifts our focus from risk to reward and increases our awareness of others who are seeking to make that opportunity a reality. As we become more aware of the opportunities to learn faster and achieve more, we may well seek out platforms that can help us do that, whether or not our institutions encourage us.

We can change our institutions too, when we join a critical mass of others within them who share our felt need for change. If we can find one or two senior leaders with the courage and conviction to support our efforts, we have a good opportunity to drive transformation of the institution by scaling the edge.

Still another path could help drive institutional change. That would be the emergence of more inspiring institutional narratives. As some institutions respond to the mounting pressure by mobilizing others around a shared opportunity, their success may help overcome some of the scalable-efficiency model's natural resistance to platforms. But again, for this to succeed, it will have to come from scaling an edge, rather than from top-down, big-bang efforts to transform the core.

The good news is that edges of large existing institutions can scale much more rapidly and with far less resources than would have been conceivable a few decades ago, thanks to the existing platform technology. All it takes is the commitment of one or two senior leaders and a few passionate people who can form the edge leadership team and take the risks required to move to a very different institutional model.

Platforms not only can provide a vehicle for scaling edges, but they also can become the foundation of the edge themselves. One of the biggest opportunities to become a large and profitable business in the decades ahead will be to design and deploy learning platforms that can help more of us learn faster together. While this is certainly not the only opportunity to address, it is worth seriously considering.

MY QUEST

As noted earlier, I've evolved my personal narrative into a call to action to others to join me on the edge, where we can collaborate in designing and deploying platforms that will help us all to achieve more of our potential. That narrative evolved as I discovered the common underlying theme of the various passions that have shaped my life. While I have been involved in the development and deployment of many kinds of platforms over the years, learning platforms are the big opportunity that excites me the most. This opportunity motivated this book, and it has motivated me to work on creating a new organization that will explicitly seek to deploy a learning platform to help more and more of us come together to achieve much more of our potential.

This new learning platform will be designed to support people as they make the journey beyond fear. It will offer workshops where participants can come together to learn how to find and cultivate their passion of the explorer and evolve their personal narrative to achieve more meaningful impact. A key goal will be to help sustain and deepen the personal connections they establish within the workshops, so they can continue to learn from each other, long after the workshops are over.

The learning platform will also encourage people to form impact groups. The participants may come from the workshops or be recruited by members via professional or other networks. The platform will provide shared workspaces where these impact groups can develop and launch initiatives that will allow them to learn through action and then reflect on the impact they achieved, so they can refine those actions to have even more impact in the future. Coaches will guide the members of these impact groups as they act and learn together.

As more and more impact groups emerge around specific domains like alternative energy technology, manufacturing operations, or woodworking, the learning platform will help them connect into broader and broader networks focused on these domains. Over time, another set of impact groups will emerge with a focus on driving fundamental change in institutions and geographies, like a specific large corporation or a city. As they come together, they will form movements, united by a shared view of the opportunity to create environments that will help more people achieve more of their potential. The learning platform will help these movements coalesce and scale.

At every level, the learning platform will be designed to encourage people to learn by acting together, reflecting on the impact of their action, and evolving their actions to achieve even more impact. Coaching services will be provided to all impact groups to help participants achieve even more impact together. Forums will be offered where people can share stories about impact achieved and seek advice or help from others beyond their own impact group. This will be an ambitious effort. At its core, the learning platform will be designed to achieve two basic objectives: first, to help participants on their personal journeys beyond fear, and second, to motivate them to come together to drive change. Since personal growth and environmental change both depend on moving people to act and learn, I call the platform an "activation center."

BOTTOM LINE

If we're going to harness the full potential of opportunity-based narratives and the passion of the explorer, we need the third pillar of positive emotion—platforms, specifically learning platforms. When we can bring all three pillars together, the opportunities will be endless. There are significant challenges, but imagine what we could accomplish with platforms that help us all to learn faster—exponentially faster.

Here are some questions to consider regarding learning platforms:

- **To what extent are the platforms you use helping you learn faster?**

- **On these platforms, are you connecting with people who are motivated to learn faster?**

- **How might you use those platforms differently to learn even faster?**

- **Do you see any untapped opportunities to develop learning platforms that support opportunity-based narratives and/or passionate explorers in particular domains?**

CONCLUSION

Transform Pressure into Passion

We're all on a journey. Some of us have thought about where we're headed, but many of us are simply following the path we have unconsciously laid out for ourselves. Many of us are attempting to pursue that path alone, but some of us are seeking help and support from others as we move forward. Most of us are feeling increasing pressure coupled with growing stress and fear as we realize that the road ahead is full of dangers. But it doesn't have to be that way.

The pressure will continue. In fact, if I'm right about the way the world is evolving, we're going to experience more and more of it over time as the pace of change accelerates. The key is how we respond to it. If we become more stressed and fearful, even the strongest and most persistent of us will eventually burn out and drop out.

THE OPPORTUNITY AHEAD

The good news is that there is an alternative. We have the opportunity to turn our stress and fear into excitement and to use that excitement as a catalyst to grow and achieve higher and higher levels of impact. Rather than burning out, our flame can burn ever brighter, lighting our way forward.

The opportunity for all of us is to achieve much more of our potential and to discover that our potential is ever expanding. We can do that by coming together with others who share our aspirations and will support us, encourage us, and challenge us in our quest to achieve more.

The isolation that many of us are feeling can be overcome. The journey we are on will become much richer and more rewarding when we find ways to make it together.

THE CHALLENGES AHEAD

What will it take for us to reach more of our potential together? First, we have to see the opportunity. As we become more consumed by fear, our ability to see opportunities in the future diminishes, even though opportunities are there, waiting to be discovered. Once we see them, we have to recognize that we cannot take them for granted. We'll have to work to achieve them, because a lot of challenges stand in our way. Pressure is mounting. All our institutions are designed to limit our potential and keep us tightly constrained, performing the tasks assigned us. Our job is to fit into the institution, rather than adapt the institution to better fit our evolving needs and aspirations. We just need to do more in less time, we're told, to relieve the growing pressure on the institution.

Our institutional cultures consider the display of vulnerability to be a sign of weakness. We're supposed to be strong and never ask for help. That contributes to the isolation that we feel.

Increasingly strident threat-based narratives play to our fear, focusing us on the enemies who are out to destroy us and eroding our sense of trust in others. (Who knows whether they are really friends or enemies in disguise?) The mass media feed our fear by focusing on the terrible things that are happening in the world. The problems seem so enormous and pervasive that we feel we can't possibly overcome them; the urge to retreat into passivity is overwhelming. At best, we gird ourselves to defend what we already have, rather than trying to achieve more.

So much of the world is consumed by pressure and fear that swimming against the current will require considerable effort. But the effort will be worthwhile. Who wants to be consumed by fear when we can accomplish so much more? We all have a hunger for hope.

THE ACTIONS WE NEED TO TAKE

Find your passion. You need to find and nurture your passion of the explorer. It is within you, waiting to be discovered, even though most of us have yet to find it. There are ways you can—and must—draw it out. Don't just wait for it to emerge, because you live in a world that is increasingly hostile to it and will do everything it can to keep you from finding it. I wish I could provide you with a step-by-step process to find it. But I can tell you how valuable that passion is.

For some of us, the passion erupts on its own, and it's impossible to ignore. But most of us have to seek it out. If you haven't yet found your passion, continue to seek new experiences and be alert to the ones that particularly excite you. Also, reflect on your life experiences, asking yourself what has stimulated you the most and given you the greatest feelings of accomplishment. Look at how you spend your time. What opportunities in the future seem to have the power to pull you in? Who do you particularly admire, and what about them do you admire?

This effort is all about looking within and without and reflecting on the emotions that people and events evoke. What makes you feel the most curiosity, excitement, admiration, and satisfaction?

Many will advise you to focus on your strengths as a way to discover your passion. I would caution against that. The key is to focus on what really excites you. If you discover your passion of the explorer and find out you don't have any particular strengths to apply in pursuit of it, don't despair. Based on my experience, I believe you will be deeply motivated by the passion of the explorer to develop those strengths, so you can achieve increasing impact in your domain. Also, you may discover different strengths that allow you to contribute in ways you hadn't imagined.

Reflect on Narratives

One promising way to draw out this passion of the explorer is to make your personal narrative explicit: write it down, and reflect on whether it really focuses you on the opportunities that inspire you to have more impact and achieve more of your potential. Also, reflect on the narratives of the institutions and geographies where you spend most of your time. Are they framing opportunities that might excite you?

Once you've found your passion, don't stop. So much remains to do. Use your awareness to evolve your personal narrative. Put into words the opportunity that your passion is driving you to address. Then find ways to make this opportunity meaningful and motivating to others, so you can frame a call to action that will draw them to you.

As you craft the call to action, identify some relatively near-term milestones that can focus the efforts of those you are calling on to help. As I discussed earlier, the most powerful narratives frame a call to action to address a large and inspiring opportunity, but they also give participants early wins, which motivate them to invest the time and effort necessary to seize the bigger opportunity.

Then reflect on the narratives that drive the environments shaping your day-to-day experiences—the institutions you spend your time in, the communities you belong to, the country you live in, and any movements you participate in. If those narratives are not aligned with your personal narrative, they will tend to limit or undermine your ability to pursue your passion and achieve more of your potential. You'll be able to accomplish so much more if you can achieve better alignment.

Evolve Your Environment

For most of us, achieving greater alignment between our personal narrative and the narratives shaping our environment will require an effort to transform our institutions and communities. Driving this change will, of course, be challenging, but the rewards will be enormous. You have the ability to evolve environments that can significantly magnify your impact and help you to achieve even more of your potential. Use it.

Connect with Others

Whatever your particular passion of the explorer might be, you will have a growing shared interest with others who have the same passion. These people can amplify your efforts. The key is to find them and come together with them in small impact groups of three to fifteen members, in which you can work together to achieve the change you need. As more people hear of your efforts, encourage them to form their own impact groups, which can collaborate with yours.

At the outset, all you need is to find a small group of people who share your particular passion and are drawn in by your personal narrative. Nurture that group. Celebrate your successes. Raise the bar in terms of further impact. Encourage each other when you run into unanticipated obstacles. Hold each other accountable when you see one another getting distracted. As you learn what you can accomplish together, you will be motivated to have even greater impact. Others will be drawn to you as they begin to see the impact you've achieved. The virtuous cycle will begin and rapidly gain speed.

Harness Platforms

In all these efforts, we need to harness the untapped potential of platforms, especially mobilization and learning platforms. These enable you to scale your efforts more quickly in ways that would have been unimaginable before the digital revolution. They can help you connect with and learn from those who share your passion, wherever in the world they reside. They can also help you connect with others who seek to drive broader institutional and social change.

Focus on Small Moves at the Beginning

As you embark on your journey from insight to action and then to impact, it's easy to become overwhelmed. It may sound like I'm saying we have to change the world from bottom to top. Well, maybe eventually, but as you move to action, remember one of my key messages: *Small moves, smartly made, can set big things in motion.*

The best way to achieve a large impact is to start small but make your moves smartly, so you can quickly learn what moves the needle. As you start to see tangible and important impacts, you will be encouraged to continue with more ambitious efforts.

That's all it takes. Embracing your passion of the explorer and evolving your personal narrative will go a long way to creating a new you. That new you will draw a small group of people who share your passion. As you see what you can accomplish together, you will be motivated to have greater impact. Others will be drawn to you, and it will snowball.

LESSONS FROM MY JOURNEY

Much of what I am sharing here is wisdom from hindsight. As I told you, I didn't find my passion of the explorer until relatively late in my own life. Part of my motivation for writing this book is the hope that it will help you find your path more quickly, so you won't have to wait as long as I did to achieve more of your potential. Here are some of the most important lessons:

- **Embrace your passion of the explorer.** The key lesson from my journey was that I waited too long to search out the underlying passion of the explorer that was driving me. I wasn't deliberately procrastinating; I simply didn't understand how significant this quest would be. My childhood experiences had instilled in me the belief that my passion or emotions were irrelevant, so I was suspicious of concepts that, like passion, have deep emotional content. Don't make that mistake.

- **Focus on opportunity.** Although I had discounted my passion, I was motivated to survive my challenging childhood. Science fiction gave me a fundamental sense of optimism that has helped me address every challenge I have faced in life and made me very responsive to opportunity. Whatever you do, don't give up hope. Find ways to hold onto a sense of opportunity, even if it is in escapist forms like novels, music, or other art forms. It will serve you well. Just keep in mind that the real world offers growing opportunities, even if your current circumstances might lead you to think otherwise.

- **Pay attention to the narratives around you.** As you seek your passion of the explorer, be alert to the

opportunity-based narratives in your environment—
personal narratives of people you know, narratives
of the institutions you interact with, broader
geographical narratives of the cities, regions, and
countries you live in or visit, and the narratives of
movements you come across and possibly belong
to. Do the opportunities framed by these narratives
excite you? Narratives of others can be a catalyst for
the discovery of your own passion of the explorer. In
my case, I was drawn across the country as a young
adult by the Silicon Valley narrative, which spoke to
me powerfully. Unfortunately, at the time, I did not
reflect enough on why this narrative had such a hold
on me. If I had, I might have discovered my passion of
the explorer and refined my personal narrative much
earlier.

- **Connect with others.** When we face challenges, we
  tend to isolate ourselves. Fight that tendency, even
  if you are an introvert like me. I initially found ways
  to connect with others through writing. That drew
  in people who encouraged and reinforced me. My
  early personal narrative focused on asking others to
  come to me with problems and issues I could solve
  with my mind. That connected me with people who
  appreciated my help and built sustaining relationships
  with me. Whether or not you have found your passion
  of the explorer, find ways to overcome isolation and
  connect, so you can receive emotional support and
  encouragement. Look especially for people with the
  passion of the explorer, because they can amplify

your energy, even if you are committed to different domains.

- **Use crises as catalysts for learning.** Personal crises can be deeply hurtful. We instinctively try to get through them as quickly as possible and move on. Resist that instinct. Instead, view crises as opportunities to learn, reflecting on what led to them and what you can do to grow as a result of the experience. As I've indicated in this book, my second divorce was a catalyst to seek out my passion of the explorer and evolve my personal narrative, but I'm not just talking about personal crises. The crisis can be a crisis in your career or a broader crisis, like the recent global pandemic. An encouraging number of people have told me the pandemic prompted them to reflect on how they were spending their time. Many of them realized that their time was being consumed by meaningless activities and that they needed to identify what would be more fulfilling.

- **Look for patterns in the past.** By looking back on my life and reflecting on it, I found the underlying passion of the explorer that had been trying to express itself. Pulling back from what had excited me at various times, I began to see what these sources of excitement had in common—a pattern that brought together these apparently divergent domains to reveal the passion that had driven me unconsciously.

- **Look ahead.** Looking to the past can be helpful, but the key is to use the insight you gain to understand what domain draws you forward, what opportunities and challenges excite you the most, and where people can be most helpful to you as you continue your journey. Don't get stuck in the past. To achieve more of your potential, you need to look ahead and discover where you want to go.

- **Evolve your personal narrative.** As I've indicated, my discovery of the real passion of the explorer that had motivated and excited me throughout my life helped me frame a personal narrative that was much more meaningful to me and, equally importantly, to the others with whom I was seeking to connect. As I pursued my passion, I further evolved my narrative based on the experience I had gained. Similarly, your personal narrative should evolve as you connect and learn.

- **Connect with emotions.** Many people who succeed in business become suspect of emotions and want everything to be rational, so they can just gather the data and do the analysis. Certainly, reason has an important role to play in the passion of the explorer, but so does emotion. Emotion not only gives you the excitement and courage to overcome fear and confront unexpected challenges, it also lets you make deeper connections with others and motivate them to help you on your journey. Embrace emotions as a key to motivating yourself, motivating others, and drawing out more of your potential. Start by looking within to understand the emotions that are driving you now: feel the fear if it is there, as it most likely is. Then cultivate the emotions that can help you overcome it.

THE BROADER CONTEXT

Much of this book has been directed to you as an individual; after all, individuals read books. As I indicated in the introduction, I was trained in business strategy, and much of my long career has focused on helping companies and other institutions evolve their strategies in rapidly changing times. One of the key insights I developed is that what really matters is psychology, not strategy. If you don't understand the psychology of the individuals involved, if you don't understand their emotions (their hopes and fears and what excites them), and if you don't understand what motivates them, your strategic plans will just be documents on a shelf. The need to understand psychology starts with individuals, then extends to the groups they form, their institutions, and the broader society they inhabit.

But let me be clear, this is not just about you. It is about us. Like it or not, we are all part of the same society, ultimately a global society that is rapidly evolving in a more connected world. I have a vested interest in having all of you embrace the opportunity I've outlined. If you don't, we are in growing peril of spiraling into a dystopian society in which fear prevails, trust erodes, and barriers to movement will, at best, hold all of us prisoners in our current circumstances. As that dynamic plays out, we try to hold onto what we have, even as those actions place everything at risk, as wars and civil strife wreak havoc on our lives.

A lot is at stake. Our institutions are under growing pressure and show signs of unraveling. Our cities and countries are polarizing as threat-based narratives play to our fears. We can't let that continue. I don't want to fall into a threat-based narrative of my own; I want to stay focused on the opportunities I've outlined, but I also want to be aware of the consequences of ignoring those opportunities.

This is in no way an us-versus-them proposition. It's all about us coming together to help each other see our shared opportunity to increase our potential and create a society and institutions that will help us achieve it. We'll achieve much more of that potential if we pursue that opportunity together than if we remain isolated, either individually or in institutional or social silos.

True, it starts with us as individuals, but it can't end there. We need to do our own work in reflecting on what led us to where we are and what emotions are driving our choices and actions. We need to draw out our passion of the explorer and evolve our personal narratives. But then we need to connect with others to evolve our institutions and societies in ways that help others discover and pursue their passion of the explorer. We need to embark on a long march through our institutions—all of them—and transform them, developing the fundamentally different institutional models and architectures necessary to unleash the potential of narratives, passion, and platforms.

We'll also need to find ways to connect people across institutions so we can address the broader social and political change required to bring everyone together, including those who are marginalized and blocked from the opportunities that many of us have enjoyed. They too have a passion of the explorer within them, waiting to be unleashed, but the quest for their next meal and a roof over their heads has often pushed it deep down and out of sight. If they can discover and cultivate that passion, we all will benefit.

The good news is that we have the tools we need to drive this change. As we individually discover our passion of the explorer, we can begin to craft narratives around broader opportunities at the institutional, geographical, or movement level that will help to motivate and mobilize others to change the world. We can then deploy and evolve platforms that will connect a growing number of participants and scale our efforts more rapidly and with less resources than we might have thought possible.

If we do this right, we will for the first time be able to move beyond the world of diminishing returns that naturally results from a scalable-efficiency mindset and move into a world where returns increase exponentially, shaped by two forces. First, more and more of us will be driven by our passion of the explorer, achieving more of our potential and being motivated to keep increasing the value we deliver to others. Second, we will have broader narratives and platforms that can unleash powerful network effects, so that value gets created more rapidly. The exponential growth in value won't just be driven by more people participating. It will ultimately be driven by our ability to learn faster together, because we can learn from each other at scale.

MY JOURNEY CONTINUES

I'm committed to making this happen. This book is just the next step on a journey that has inspired and excited me for decades. I will now shift my focus to building and scaling a learning platform that will help bring more and more of us together to overcome fear and develop the excitement that will motivate us to achieve much more of our potential. We not only need to change ourselves; we also need to rebuild our institutions, economies, and societies so that they encourage everyone to make this journey. The platform I am seeking to build will help us on both fronts.

I hope many readers, including you, will be interested in participating in the programs I will be developing to help us move beyond fear and cultivate the passion of the explorer. Beyond that, I hope that you will be interested in helping me design and develop those programs, as well as the platform that will connect more and more participants in their quest to achieve impact that matters. I cannot do this alone. I need your help.

If you are interested in joining me on this journey, please go to my website at www.johnhagel.com and sign up, so I can keep you posted on this initiative as it unfolds. In one way or another, I hope we can stay connected as we address the opportunities ahead of us.

BOTTOM LINE

This is too big an opportunity to pass up. It starts with you but ultimately requires all of us to find our passion of the explorer, evolve our personal narratives, and participate in learning platforms so we can address opportunities that are bigger than any of us could hope to achieve on our own. That's the only way to make the journey beyond fear and turn pressure into potential. The ball is in your court:

- **What will you do?**

- **What choices will you make?**

- **What actions will you take?**

- **Who will you connect with to achieve even more impact?**

ACKNOWLEDGMENTS

Acknowledgements for a book of this type are challenging since it is about my life's journey as well as research that I have pursued with others over many decades. If I were to acknowledge everyone who contributed to the ideas and insights in this book, that would become a book of its own.

As a result, let me just single out a few people along the way who played a particularly prominent role in shaping my journey. Of course, I would want to start with my mother and father, as well as my sister. We went through so much together, and my path has been significantly influenced by the roles they played in my life. On this front, I would also want to call out my two stepdaughters, Rachel Rosenfelt and Rebecca Rosenfelt, since they played a major role in my life and I learned so much by being able to support their journey.

In my professional life, I have benefited from the support and encouragement of many mentors, but I would single out the following as having played a particularly influential role in shaping my evolving personal narrative: Bruce Henderson at Boston Consulting Group, Carter Bales at McKinsey & Co., and Eric Openshaw at Deloitte.

I have collaborated with many people throughout my career, but perhaps my longest standing and most productive collaboration has been with John Seely Brown. JSB, as he is known, was the head of the Palo Alto Research Center and former Chief Scientist at Xerox. JSB joined me as co-founder and co-chairman of the Center for the Edge research center at Deloitte. We come from very different backgrounds and perspectives, but our collaboration has been instrumental in shaping my view of the Big Shift and the profound impact it is having on institutions around the world.

My assistant, Carrie Howell, has supported me on my journey for decades. Without her, I would have been overwhelmed so many times. Her unrelenting support has helped to motivate me to keep on venturing out onto the edge so that I can continue to have more and more impact. I am so grateful that we connected and have stayed connected for such a long period. I look forward to continuing our collaboration for many years to come.

My agent, Jim Levine, was very helpful in bringing this book to life. I also am indebted to a number of editors, including Amy Li, Arthur Goldwag, and Steve Straus, who helped me to sharpen the text and make it even more readable and compelling. Of course, without the collaboration with McGraw Hill, this book would still be sitting in my computer.

While grateful for the support and stimulation of so many people throughout my life, I must ultimately take full responsibility for the perspectives that I am sharing in this book. There's a lot of risk in sharing so much personal information and venturing out into uncharted territories, but it is exciting and I have learned so much in the process of writing this book. My perspectives will undoubtedly continue to evolve, but I welcome the opportunity to share with you some of the lessons that I have learned so far. More to come.

INDEX

ABOUT THE AUTHOR

John Hagel III has more than 40 years' experience as a management consultant, author, speaker, and entrepreneur. After recently retiring from Deloitte, he plans to establish a new Center that will develop a series of programs to help people make the journey beyond fear. John has founded a new company, Beyond Our Edge, LLC, that works with companies and people who are seeking to anticipate the future and achieve much greater impact.

While at Deloitte, John was the founder and chairman of the Silicon Valley–based Deloitte Center for the Edge, focusing on identifying emerging business opportunities that are not yet on the CEO's agenda. Before joining Deloitte, John was an independent consultant and writer, and prior to that was a principal at McKinsey & Company and a leader of their Strategy Practice as well as the founder of their E-Commerce Practice. John has served as senior vice president of strategy at Atari, Inc., and is the founder of two Silicon Valley startups.

John is also a faculty member at Singularity University, where he gives frequent talks on the mounting performance pressure created by digital technology and promising approaches to help traditional companies make the transition from a linear to an exponential world. He is also on the board of trustees at the Santa Fe Institute, an organization that conducts leading-edge research on complex adaptive systems. He has also led a number of initiatives regarding business transformation with the World Economic Forum.

John is the author of *The Power of Pull*, published by Basic Books in April 2010. He is also the author of a series of bestselling business books, *Net Gain*, *Net Worth*, *Out of the Box*, and *The Only Sustainable Edge*. He is widely published and quoted in major business publications including *The Economist*, *Fortune*, *Forbes*, *Business Week*, *Financial Times*, and *Wall Street Journal*, as well as general media like the *New York Times*, NBC and BBC. He has won two awards from *Harvard Business Review* for best articles in that publication and has been recognized as an industry thought leader by a variety of publications and institutions, including the World Economic Forum and *Business Week*.

John has his own website at www.johnhagel.com, and for many years wrote personal blogs at www.edgeperspectives .typepad.com, and also contributes postings on the Harvard Business Review, Fortune, and Techonomy websites. He is active in social media and can be followed on Twitter at @jhagel and on LinkedIn at https://www.linkedin.com/in/jhagel/.

John holds a BA from Wesleyan University, a B.Phil. from Oxford University, and a JD and MBA from Harvard University.